D0110332

I'd Rather Teach Peace

Colman McCarthy

ORBIS BOOKS

Maryknoll, New York 10545

Founded in 1970, Orbis Books endeavors to publish works that enlighten the mind, nourish the spirit, and challenge the conscience. The publishing arm of the Maryknoll Fathers & Brothers, Orbis seeks to explore the global dimensions of the Christian faith and mission, to invite dialogue with diverse cultures and religious traditions, and to serve the cause of reconciliation and peace. The books published reflect the views of their authors and do not represent the official position of the Maryknoll Society. To learn more about Maryknoll and Orbis Books, please visit our website at www.maryknoll.org.

Manufactured in the United States of America.
Manuscript editing and typesetting by Joan Weber Laflamme.

Library of Congress Cataloging-in-Publication Data

McCarthy, Colman.
    I'd rather teach peace / Colman McCarthy.
      p. cm.
    ISBN 978-1-57075-762-4
    1. Peace—Study and teaching—Washington Metropolitan Area. I. Title.
JZ5534 .M33 2002
303.6'6—dc21

                2002000624

*For Mav McCarthy,
my teacher of the important lessons,
and to my former and current students,
more than five thousand now,
from Abbey to Zulima*

Contents

Acknowledgments vi
Preface to the Paperback Edition viii
Preface xi

SEPTEMBER
Don't Ask Questions, Question the Answers 1
 Georgetown Law 1
 Oak Hill Youth Center, Laurel, Maryland 5
 The Washington Center 8
 Stone Ridge Sacred Heart School for Girls,
   Bethesda, Maryland 9
 University of Maryland 15
 School Without Walls 16

OCTOBER
Give the World Your Best, Anyway 18
 University of Maryland 18
 School Without Walls 22
 Stone Ridge 24
 Oak Hill 30
 Georgetown Law 32
 The Washington Center 38

NOVEMBER
Ideas to Practice, Not Mull 44
 Stone Ridge 44
 The Washington Center 51
 University of Maryland 54
 Georgetown Law 65
 Oak Hill 75
 School Without Walls 79

DECEMBER
Power With, Not Power Over   **89**
    Stone Ridge   89
    School Without Walls   94
    Georgetown Law   95
    The Washington Center   111
    University of Maryland   115
    Oak Hill   118

SEMESTER'S END
A Few of the Many Who "Got It"   **122**
    Tara Lee   123
    Jim McGovern   124
    Chappell Marmon   127
    Lexie Tillotson   129
    Fred Werner   131

Epilogue   **133**
    Bernie Shulman   133
    Marye Eroh   136

Select Bibliography on Peace   **138**

Acknowledgments

From time to time I have asked my students to keep journals during the semester, as a way to keep firm their commitment to learning and to keep an eye open for the occasional idea or moment that sparkles. One year a student blessed with the kind of audacity that energizes a class raised her hand to ask me, "And will you be keeping a journal, too?" I tried dodging that little zinger with a puny pun: "I'm exempt. All I do is journal. I'm a journal-ist." While withstanding the groaning that followed, I knew the student had a point.

My thanks to her for asking a question I can now answer with an unevasive yes. I am grateful to my students in the fall semester of 2000 at the Oak Hill Youth Prison, Georgetown Law, The University of Maryland, Stone Ridge, Landon, Holton-Arms, Holy Child, St. Andrews, School Without Walls, and the Washington Center for Internships for being all any teacher could want: open-minded and willing to take intellectual risks. I have appreciated the kindness of the deans and principals at those schools for inviting me to their classrooms. The first faculty person to welcome me—in 1982—to a school was Phyllis Weiss, an all-star literature teacher at School Without Walls in Washington, who is now approaching her fortieth year of high school teaching.

My courses on nonviolence are an extension of my work at the Center for Teaching Peace, a small non-profit in Washington that my wife, Mavourneen, and I began in 1985 and which our three children have been involved with as teachers. The much appreciated supporters of the Center have included the Helen Sperry Lea Foundation, the Olender

Foundation, the Florence and John Schumann Foundation, the Morris and Gwendolyn Cafritz Foundation, the Public Welfare Foundation, the Streisand Foundation, the Peace Development Fund, Sargent Shriver, Linda Smith, Polly Steinway, Katherine Hessler, John Stohrm and the large numbers of subscribers to the Center's newsletter, *Peace Times*.

To these, and others, my thanks for holding fast to the idea that the peaceable society is not only possible, it is inevitable—if we press on, starting today. Tomorrow is too late.

Preface to the Paperback Edition

Six years after the original publication in hardcover, this paperback edition arrives at a moment when peace education appears to be taking hold and, often enough, taken seriously. It comes also when the American invasion of Iraq has proved to be as recklessly violent and politically fruitless as I and many others said it would.

Much of my work, aside from classroom teaching, is communicating with other teachers on efforts they might be making to create peace classes in their local schools. Signs of progress appear, as in this recent letter.

Dear Colman,

I am an English teacher at Niles West High School in Skokie, a suburb just north of Chicago. I'm writing to let you know that our district, somewhat miraculously, approved a peace studies course. Here is the full story.

I have had a lifelong interest in peace studies and peace education. . . . Due to your book I'd Rather Teach Peace *I had the idea of starting a peace course in our district. I ordered your two collections of peace essays several years ago, and you wrote back an encouraging letter.*

It takes a long time to get a course started here, with many institutional hoops to jump through. Two other teachers and I put a proposal together which at first was rejected. It was too "social studies" oriented. We are all, incidentally, English teachers. Our second proposal, titled "The Literature of Peace," was accepted by the school board. This was the miraculous part.

Because the course is part of the English curriculum, we will be teaching more literature—poetry, short stories, drama—than you would in yours.

We begin teaching the course this fall. With two high schools in our district, we will have one course in each. I would love to keep in touch with you as we go through this process. The three of us are new at this, and we want to do the best we can to make sure the courses become popular and continue. I would love to see them blossom into a school-wide peace studies program involving our entire curriculum. We are at the first step.

The writer of the letter is Paul Wack, a teacher who has put into practice the memorable thought of Eleanor Roosevelt: "Some of us are dreamers and some of us are doers. But what the world really needs are dreamers who do and doers who dream."

I wrote back to Paul: "Until I check the AAU indoor record book for the fastest time anyone has created a peace studies course, I'm guessing you are close to medaling. It's usually years and years between a proposal and the day students walk into a class devoted to studying and discussing peace. . . . You've done well in Skokie. But watch out. The trouble with a good idea is that it soon degenerates into hard work. Enjoy your degeneracy!"

Creating a foothold for peace education—whether in elementary, middle, or high schools, or colleges and universities—almost always is traceable to one singularly resolute person who says, "this will happen and I'll make it happen." Despite the media's continually depicting the peace movement as little more than antiwar rallies or protestors still sticking flower in gun barrels, it is much more. There are the many lovers of long shots—students, teachers, principals, school superintendents, parents—who value studying nonviolence as the sane, moral, and effective alternative to violence in all its forms: military violence, environmental violence, emotional violence, verbal violence, domestic violence, racial violence, gender-based violence, corporate violence, economic violence, institutional violence, religious violence, bullying violence, and violence against animals.

What Paul Wack pulled off in Skokie, Jeremy Fischer did in Bethesda, Maryland. I came to know him a decade ago after speaking at a student assembly at his high school, Walter Johnson, and calling on students to act on the ideal of Peter Kropotkin, the Russian anarchist and pacifist: "Think about the kind of world you want to live and work in. What do you need to build that world? Demand that your teachers teach you that."

After the assembly, Jeremy Fischer, a ninth grader, skipped his next class to talk with me. Did I have a reading list for books on nonviolence? He wanted to know about groups I had praised in my speech: the War Resisters League, Pax Christi, the Catholic Worker, the Fellowship of Reconciliation. I invited him to enroll in one of my summer courses, which he did during consecutive summers, bringing along his father, a teacher, both times.

Jeremy the ninth grader became a demander in the Kropotkin mold. With gritty persistence, he wrote letters to school officials. He phoned them. He sought out teachers. He endured brush-offs, runarounds, frowns, yawns, and countless can't-you-see-I'm-busy looks from finger-tapping faculty rajahs. But he didn't go away. He had learned to hang on, hang in, hang out—but never to hang it up. A payoff came. In the spring semester of his senior year at Walter Johnson—his ninth inning of high school—Jeremy found Ty Healy, a sympathetic faculty member ready to teach the peace course. It has been in place for the past ten years.

When we think of the world's heralded peacemakers—the Gandhis, Kings, Yunuses, Perez Esquivels, and Corrigans—let us remember also the Paul Wacks and Jeremy Fischers. Perhaps they didn't do great things, but—just as important—they did small things in a great way.

—Colman McCarthy
September 2007

Preface

In early spring 1982 an English teacher at School Without Walls, a District of Columbia public high school where two of my children were students, invited me to speak to her class on the techniques of writing. At the time I had been a columnist for *The Washington Post* for fourteen years and would be for another fourteen. Five blocks from the White House—no school is closer—"Walls," as its three hundred students call it, specializes in experiential as well as theoretical learning. Study zoology by interning at the National Zoo, or politics by working one day a week in a congressional office, or drama by volunteering at the Kennedy Center.

After speaking to the English literature class about writing, I told the teacher how enjoyable her students were during the give-and-take discussion. I mentioned, too, my satisfaction in being with them, a therapeutic break from the solitariness of writing. It wasn't banter. I meant it. The exhilaration was real. The teacher, seasoned and skilled in bluff-calling, said that if I really found the visit to her class so enlivening, why not come back in the fall to offer my own course. Go beyond gushing, was her message.

"You could teach writing," she said. Impulsively I replied, "I'd rather teach peace."

Months later, in the opening week of the fall semester, I was in a Walls classroom as a volunteer teacher with twenty-five students. The course, based on the literature of peace, was titled "Solutions to Violence." We met weekly from 1 P.M. to 3:30 P.M. I made up the time at the *Post* by not taking lunch breaks during the week, not that anyone much noticed. Who cares where columnists spend their hours as long as the copy comes in on time.

Journalistically, I was creating my own education beat. Classroom teaching was my legwork. Instead of waiting for the Brookings Institution or the Heritage Foundation to issue still another report from the shallow end of the think tank on the state of American education—dismal, predictably—and then writing a column on the findings of the alleged experts, I could ignore their gab and draw on my own experiences in a public school. I could seek an answer to a question that had long gripped me: Can peacemaking be taught—and learned? If peace is what every government claims to be seeking, and if peace is what every human heart yearns for, could it have a place in our school curricula?

Educationally, I learned that my students were hungry to explore the unknown landscape of pacifism, nonviolence, and peaceful conflict resolution. I learned also, and a bit unsettlingly, that I was equally hungry to teach it. I was in my mid-forties, ready to diversify intellectually and see what unused brain cells might be activated.

A balance was created between my writing life and my teaching life: one was thinking in private meant for a large reading audience, the other was thinking in public for a small give-and-take audience—those twenty-five students I spent that year with. They were open-minded, spirited, and appreciative, a bracing mix of dreamers, skeptics, dolts, and doves. Many were from low-income neighborhoods and saw Walls as an escape route from poverty. Some came from moneyed families—second and third generation escapees—that had ample funds for private schools but not a liking for the insularity.

The course went well. I returned for a second and third year. After establishing the course at Walls, I turned the class over to a succession of college students that I trained. They were welcomed by a principal who believed that a person's passion for education meant more than a folder of teaching certificates. I took the course to another D.C. high school—Woodrow Wilson—and stayed two years. I turned the course over to my son Jim, a recent Notre Dame graduate, and then to another son, John, a baseball coach and former minor league knuckleball pitcher who has taught the course for the past eight years as a volunteer.

In 1987, with Walls and Wilson in place, I was invited to teach at a suburban Washington school. Once again I had been challenged by an educator to stop talking and begin doing. I had given a speech to an annual conference of Maryland high school principals and assistant principals. "Why aren't you offering courses on the history, theory, and practice of nonviolence?" I asked. During the Q&A, a principal said she would like to put a course in place "if you'll come teach it." The next semester I was volunteering for a daily 7:30 A.M. class at Bethesda–Chevy Chase High School.

The same year Robert Pitofsky, dean of Georgetown University Law Center, welcomed my proposal to design and teach a course called "Law, Conscience, and Nonviolence." A year earlier I had begun offering a similar course in the General Honors Program at the University of Maryland. In 1995 the Washington Center for Internships and Academic Seminars, an educational non-profit that brings college students to the capital for a semester, invited me to teach an evening class. The next year I left the *Post* to give full time to my students. I added one more class—a year-round seminar on nonviolence at a juvenile prison, the Oak Hill Youth Center in Laurel, Maryland. During summers I kept the Washington Center course going, as well as a six-week mini-course for college students interning in the city.

By rough estimate I've had more than five thousand students since that first high school class. I've felt blessed. With all of them, from the brainiest third year law students on their way to six figure beginning salaries on K Street to fourteen-year-old illiterates locked up for hustling drugs, I emphasized one theme: alternatives to violence exist and, if individuals and nations can organize themselves properly, nonviolent force is always stronger, more enduring, and assuredly more moral than violent force.

Some students opened their minds to this immediately. They understood Gandhi: "Nonviolence is the weapon of the strong." They believed King: "The choice is not between violence and nonviolence but between nonviolence and nonexistence."

Other students have had doubts, which I encouraged them to express. They did, repeatedly. Nonviolence and pacifism are beautiful theories and ideals, they said, but in the real world, where muggers and international despots lurk, let's keep our fists cocked and our bomb bays open.

All I asked of the realists was that they think about this: Do you depend on violent force or nonviolent force to create peace? Not just peace in some vague "out there," but peace in our homes, where physical beatings are the leading cause of injury among American women, or peace in the developing world, where some thirty-five thousand children die every day from preventable diseases, or peace in those parts of the world where more than 40,000 people die every month in some thirty-five wars or conflicts—mostly the poor killing the poor—or peace where the U.S. Congress gives $700 million a day to the Pentagon, which is $8,000 a second and three times the Peace Corps budget for a year.

If violence were effective, peace would have reigned eons ago.

At all schools my course was based on the literature of peace—the writings of past and current peacemakers. I created my own textbook—*Solutions to Violence*—which runs deep with sixteen chapters that include Gandhi, Tolstoy, Dorothy Day, Gene Sharp, Jeannette Rankin, Joan Baez, Isaac Bashevis Singer, Sargent Shriver, Jane Addams, Carol Ascher, Helen Nearing, and Daniel Berrigan, and ranges from nonviolent resistance to the Holocaust to animal rights. The book was published by the Center for Teaching Peace. With generous foundation support, our work is to help schools at all levels offer courses on the methods, practitioners, effectiveness, and history of nonviolent conflict resolution. In my classes, essays are read, discussed, and debated. My goal has been not to tell students what to think but how to think: gather as much information as possible about nonviolence and then either embrace or reject it. I went with the thought of Peter Kropotkin, the Russian anarchist who advised students in *Mutual Aid:* "Think about the kind of world you want to live and work in. What do you need to build that world? Demand that your teachers teach you that."

The students I've been with these twenty years are looking for a world where it becomes a little easier to love and a lot harder to hate, where learning nonviolence means that we dedicate our hearts, minds, time, and money to a commitment that the force of love, the force of truth, the force of justice, and the force of organized resistance to corrupt power are seen as sane and the force of fists, guns, armies, and bombs insane.

Over the years other teachers have suggested that I offer what they call "balance" in my courses, that I give students "the other side." I'm never sure exactly what that means. After assigning students to read Gandhi, should I have them also read von Clausewitz? After Martin Luther King's essay against the Vietnam War, Colin Powell's memoir favoring the Persian Gulf War? After Justice William Brennan's and Thurgood Marshall's views opposing the death penalty, George W. Bush's and Saddam Hussein's favoring it? After a woman's account of using a nonviolent defense against a rapist, the thwarted rapist's side?

What I have surety about is that students come into my classes already well educated, often overeducated, in the ethic of violence. The educators? The nation's long-tenured cultural faculty: political leaders who fund wars and send the young to fight them, judges and juries who dispatch people to death row, filmmakers who script gunplay movies and cartoons, toy manufacturers marketing "action games," parents in war-zone homes where verbal or physical abuse is common, high-school history texts that tell about Calamity Jane but not Jane Addams, Daniel Boone but not Daniel Berrigan.

I can't in conscience teach the other side. Students have already been saturated with it. No, I say, *my* course is the other side. With me they will have a chance to examine solutions and alternatives to violence. The course is still well short of offering balance. One semester in twelve or sixteen or more years of education is a pittance, not a balance.

Peace education is in its infancy. In 1988 our Center gave fifteen thousand dollars in seed money to a university to create a peace studies program. In the spring of 2001 a major in peace studies was established, thanks to one professor and some students who doggedly kept demanding, as Kropotkin counseled. The effort took thirteen years, a speed record in higher education, I was told. In the 1990s I needed six years to persuade officials in Montgomery County, Maryland—school board members, curriculum committees, principals and assorted desk barons—to approve my text *Solutions to Violence* for use in schools, including the one where I had been volunteering for twelve years. This was a supposedly enlightened, progressive county. Once a school board member, who presented himself as politically astute, said I would do well to come up with another name besides peace studies. *Studies* was all right, but *peace* might alarm some parents. I envisioned a newspaper headline: "Proposed Peace Course Threatens Community Stability."

As a lifelong pacifist, my early hunches are regularly confirmed. Yes, peacemaking can be taught, the literature is large and growing. Yes, the young are passionately seeking alternatives to violence. Yes, our schools should be educating as much about peacemakers as peacebreakers. Yes, whether the killing and harming are done by armies, racists, corporations, polluters, domestic batterers, street thugs or boardroom thugs, terrorists, schoolyard bullies, animal exploiters, or others in this graceless lot, the cycle of violence can be broken—but only if choices are laid out, starting in the nation's seventy-eight thousand elementary schools, thirty-one thousand high schools, and three thousand colleges.

In twenty years I've seen the issue of violence in the schools surface as a major public-policy debate. Solutions range from metal detectors and police in the hallways to national conferences on youth violence. Suddenly we are awash with experts overflowing with opinions and strategies. As a journalist for thirty-five years, I don't believe half of what they say, and of the other half I have grave doubts. As a classroom teacher, my experienced-based belief is that unless we teach our children peace someone else will teach them violence.

During my two decades of teaching peace, wars and conflicts have been fought in all parts of the world. My classroom discussions regularly focused on them, especially when America was militarily involved. As I write now—two months after September 11, 2001—advocates for pacifism are all but ignored, their arguments for a nonviolent response to terrorist attacks derided as not only unrealistic but unpatriotic. This is a time for a show of force, it is declared by U.S. political and military leaders, with the mainstream clergy dutifully praying that God continue to bless America. As retribution hysteria grows, and at least $20 billion more is found to lubricate an already over-oiled war machine, it is forgotten that pacifists stoutly believe in the use of force, too. Moral force, the force of organized resistance to violence, the force of sharing wealth, and the force of dialogue, compromise and negotiation.

After September 11, my students came to class with one main question: What does the United States do now? We examined the four possible solutions: military, political, legal, and moral.

The military option, predictably, was chosen by Congress and the Bush administration. The pattern was familiar: theorize, demonize, victimize, rationalize. Theorizing began on September 11. Who attacked America, and why? It was evildoers, easily demonized. Get them dead or alive. Then the victimizing began: pilots from the world's richest nation bombing people in one of the world's poorest. In Washington, the violence is rationalized.

The political solution was to follow the advice the Bush administration regularly gives to the Israeli government and the Palestine Liberation Organization: stop the killing, meet with each other, negotiate, compromise, and dialogue. For eight years, the Clinton administration preached that same message to the factions in Northern Ireland. After the Columbine High School massacre in April 1999, President Clinton told a high school peer mediation group: "We must do more to reach out to our children and teach them to express their anger and resolve their conflicts with words, not weapons."

If we tell others to settle their differences this way, why not follow our own advice? In the early 1970s, Richard Nixon began a dialogue with the Chinese Communists. Ronald Reagan did the same with the Soviet Union, which he had once demonized as "the evil empire." In time, both these former enemies—their weapons aimed at us and ours at them—became trading partners. The political force of dialogue was potent.

The legal option was on display in the World Court at The Hague, where Slobodan Milosevic, finally but inevitably tracked down, was on trial and getting due process—of the same stripe as that of a federal court in New York that gave life sentences to terrorists found guilty of the first attack on the World Trade Center.

The moral solution would have been to say to those behind September 11, we forgive you, and then ask them to forgive us for all of our violence, and proceed to do the hard toil of reconciliation. The notion of mutual forgiveness is from the Lord's Prayer, recited by Bush, his generals, and assorted clergy at the National Cathedral three days after the attacks. But it was all for show. After the ceremony, Senator John McCain defined the link between church and state: "Pray first, then fight."

After September 11, a few students asked what they could do as a personal response. Class discussions were among the most heartfelt I have ever witnessed. A range of options were offered, some by me, some by students. Try to simplify your life. Figure out the difference between what you want and what you need. Decrease consumption of goods and services that rely heavily on oil, either to transport them to the marketplace or to keep them working after purchase. Deny money to companies that profit from violence, from weapons sellers to film studios to the meat industry. Do a favor for someone who cannot thank you. Know that a truly revolutionary act is to raise decent and generous children. Tell others you love them. Join groups that advocate nonviolence: the Fellowship of Reconciliation, Pax Christi, the War Resisters League, the Catholic Worker, Feminists for Life, Public Citizen. Subscribe to magazines that deliver the news of social justice, nonviolence and civil resistance. Remember the thought of Jim Douglass: "The first thing to be disrupted by our commitment to nonviolence will not be the system but our own lives." For more sustenance, there is Gandhi's belief: "It is the law of love that rules mankind. Had violence, i.e. hate, ruled us, we should have become extinct long ago. And yet, the tragedy of it is that the so-called civilized men and nations conduct themselves as if the basis of society was violence."

I have been invited to hundreds of schools—at all levels, from pre-K to doctoral programs—to speak on nonviolence and do workshops on the methods of conflict management. At every school I have found students, teachers, and administrators ready to embrace the idea of peace education. But turning an idea into a fact is where dreamers and doers separate. There's an old Irish saying—and it usually is—that goes like this: The trouble with a good idea is that it soon degenerates into hard work. The degeneracy involves rallying support for academic courses on pacifism—the belief—and nonviolence—the method—and then pushing to have those courses as valued as math, science, languages, literature, and sports. The hard work gets harder at budget time. When a teacher proposes peace courses to an administrator, the first thought in the administrator's mind is, "What will this cost?" He or she is thinking money, the teacher is thinking reform. Guess which wins? Oddly, money has been found for metal detectors. Money has been found for hallway police.

It's been found for ID badges that students and faculties are now required to wear at many schools. It's been found to pay for administrators to fly off to yet another national conference on youth violence where the inevitable cry will be heard, "Something must be done!"

I had a student at the University of Maryland a while back who wrote a thirteen-word paper that for both brevity and breadth—the rarest of combinations—has stayed with me: "Q. Why are we violent but not illiterate? A. Because we are taught to read." This student—an imaginative lad named David Allan, who went on to serve in Teach for America and is now a writer in San Francisco—didn't know it but he shared the genius of both Albert Einstein and Mohandas Gandhi. Einstein wrote: "We must begin to inoculate our children against militarism by educating them in the spirit of pacifism, . . . I would teach peace rather than war, love rather than hate." Gandhi: "If we are to reach real peace in the world, we shall have to begin with the children. And if they will grow up in their natural innocence, we won't have to struggle, we won't have to pass fruitless resolutions, but we shall go from love to love and peace to peace."

The following pages tell part of the story of my teaching courses on peace at six schools in the fall semester of 2000. Journaled month by month, from September through December, and school by school, it is part reporting, part reflection, and part an exploration of human possibilities. What should be the moral purpose of writing if not to test ideals that can help fulfill the one possibility we all hope for, the peaceable society? For me, any other kind of writing would be menial. Why bother?

For me, teaching any subject other than peace would be tramping through an intellectual desert. The earth is too small a planet and we too brief visitors for anything to matter more than the struggle for peace.

September

Don't Ask Questions, Question the Answers

To find the way to make peace with ourselves and to offer it to others, both spiritually and politically, is the most important kind of learning. To accept our abilities and limitations, and the differences in others—this is the contentment that gives life its highest value. It frees us to grow without restraint and to settle without pressure.

—WENDY SCHWARTZ

The job of the peacemaker is to stop war, to purify the world, to get it saved from poverty and riches, to heal the sick, to comfort the sad, to wake up those who have not yet found God, to create joy and beauty wherever you go.

—MURIEL LESTER

Georgetown Law

Martin Buber said that "all real living is meeting." Opening classes are for that. Sixteen second- and third-year students have signed on. Some years the number has been twenty. Others twelve. In the catalogue the course title—"Law, Conscience, and Nonviolence"—is something less than a grabber for those hot to make partner in ten years. Their yen is for boardroom law, fixer law, insider law, loophole law. After a decade or so of seventy- and eighty-hour work weeks,

1

wearied and torn, they may ask themselves, what for? Between the ages of thirty and forty-five, lawyers as a profession have the highest rate of career shifts.

When my law students go out every fall to interview for jobs at firms for the following summer, they tell me that managing partners almost always look at the courses on the transcript, and ask: "What's this one all about, this 'Law, Conscience, and Nonviolence?' That's actually a course?" A brow is furrowed: hire summer associates with a conscience? The students squirm. Damn. All was going well until then. They think fast. They say their sweetheart was in the class, and that was the only time to see each other—amid eight hours a day of studying torts, taxes, evidence, and corporate law. "Yes, yes," says the MP. Understandable. Resourceful, too.

I use the first class to relax everyone. Socialize a bit. Lower law-school intensity a half notch. Introduce ourselves, share a few stories, have a laugh or two. It's OK to be human in law school.

Going around the room, I ask students about their educational backgrounds. The first ones say, "Yale, Chapel Hill, Stanford."

"No, no," I say. "Where did you go to elementary school?" The question throws them. Elementary school? They have to think, remembering.

I want them to think and remember. We spend eight years of our lives in kindergarten, first grade, second grade, and on up during the most formative time of our lives when more than 80 percent of our character is formed, and rarely are we asked about it. I ask, "Who was your favorite grade school teacher? Have you any friends from those days? Did you think about being a lawyer in third grade?" Soon, the class is enjoying this but all the time wondering what oddity of a professor this is to be dwelling on elementary school. Maybe he's leading up to a BIG POINT, as shifty law profs like to do!

No point, large or small. Just a bias. I explain. I believe that elementary school teachers do the heavy lifting of American education. Yet few rewards go their way. The plums are reserved for college and university professors. They are well paid. They are asked by newspaper editors to review the latest books in their field, often written by other professors. They are asked to write op-eds on school reform. They are given teaching assistants to handle the lowly chores of grading papers. They enjoy paid sabbaticals.

Little of the professorial life compares with the daily arduousness of what most elementary school teachers endure. The best have courage and inner resilience the rest of us can only imagine. Under the rubric of "classroom teaching," they are expected to discipline, entertain, correct, nurse, motivate, grade, call parents, fill out attendance sheets, do lunch room duty, tell kids not to run in the hall, and tell them again the next day, and the next, find lost raincoats and boots, put chairs back in place, order books, hustle for book shelves, and then go home to turn on the evening news to behold still another politician blasting the schools for failing.

I admire elementary school teachers immensely. I urge everyone in the class to take a few minutes in the coming week to write a letter to a former grade school teacher who is remembered with affection and say thanks.

By now everyone is relaxed and then some. The class wit has been identified. The class orator, too, along with the quiet ones who by the end of the course will be doing more talking than they dreamed.

Georgetown Law is the country's largest law school, with more than fifteen hundred students and eight thousand applicants a year. My tiny class—hundreds sign up every semester for corporate law courses two floors below—attracts students who are shopping around for a philosophy of the law, not merely a career in it. I try to ground them in Gandhi, who believed in reconciliation law, not adversarial law. During his early years as a lawyer in South Africa, he wrote:

> My joy was boundless. I had learnt the true practice of law. I had learnt to find out the better side of human nature and to enter men's hearts. I realized that the true function of a lawyer was to unite parties riven asunder. The lesson was indelibly burnt into me that a large

part of my time during the twenty years of my practice
as a lawyer was occupied in bringing about private
compromises of hundreds of cases. I lost nothing
thereby—not even money, certainly not my soul.

We read this aloud and discuss it. Many in the class had no idea that Gandhi was a lawyer, and some were totally unfamiliar with him in any way. Maybe it's time for the companies that charge people up to one thousand dollars for LSAT review courses to throw in a few sample questions on Gandhi's legal theory.

For some educational theory I offer the notion of the Four A's, the stages of intellectual development through which all us move, regardless of the subject.

- *Awareness*, as when we first learn that 2+2=4, or when we first hear Gandhi's line that the "goal of reconciliation is not to bring adversaries to their knees but to their senses."
- *Acceptance*. We accept that 2+2=4, or that Gandhi was right.
- *Absorption*. An idea is taken into our lives, we need it to get by or to go on, it becomes part of us.
- *Action*. Now the game begins.

I remember standing amid fifteen thousand fellow runners at the noon start of the Boston Marathon one year, on that thin downhill country lane sloping out of Hopkinton. All morning we had been in the local school gym staying warm and gabbing to each other about other races in other times. When the starter's whistle went off, a person next to me—he looked to be over seventy and wore shorts with a dozen patches from past Bostons that he'd finished—called out, "Action time. Cut the baloney and run."

I have no clue at which A any member of the class is in. Probably a mix. Some have only a slight awareness of nonviolence, and a few may be well into the action stage. By the end of the course, we'll know more.

After mentioning a few procedural matters—the school's requirement of a six-thousand-word paper for the course, the granting of sixty-day extensions—I make a request. No one is allowed to ask questions in this class. Questions are absolutely forbidden. Instead, do something bolder, braver, and riskier: question the answers. What answers? The ones given by anyone—political leaders, the clergy, teachers, family members, friends—who says the answer to violence is more violence. To question that answer is to risk scorn, to be labeled naive. It also means questioning the nature of laws, because, to start with the United States, violence has been legalized. It is constitutional to hire a military and pay its members to solve conflicts by obeying orders to kill or threaten to kill people. Executions on death row are sanctioned both by federal and state courts. It is legal to require citizens to pay taxes that fund these and other forms of official death-dealing with no regard that a pacifist could, in conscience, want to be taxed only for nonviolent programs.

Class time is only two hours. It's not much. We could spend a full semester on Gandhi's life and thoughts alone, beginning with his statement to the sentencing judge in the great trial of 1922. For the following week I ask everyone to read the chapter on Dorothy Day, the co-founder of the *Catholic Worker* and, like Gandhi, a lawbreaker and jailbird. Before leaving, I tell the class that I'd be grateful if they would work on two assignments: (1) Don't let a day go by without telling someone you love them; and (2) write a letter to someone to whom you owe a favor. Maybe that elementary school teacher.

Oak Hill Youth Center, Laurel, Maryland

It's called a youth center, but from the two rows of razor wire atop twenty-foot chain-link fences that go for about a mile around seventy acres of rural property, it's clear it is a prison. The inmates are nearly all black teenagers sent here by District of Columbia Superior Court judges. The name Oak Hill has become synonymous with mismanagement, failed hopes, and few positive results. One administration after another has come in with hopes of reform and then left with conditions worse. In the mid-1990s Oak Hill was placed in receivership by the Superior Court, which meant administrative decisions would have to be reviewed by a judge. The education program was turned over to a pair of professors from the University of Maryland's school of education. I heard about it and in the summer of 1998 offered to come out—a sixty-mile round trip and over fifty traffic lights, most unco-ordinated—to teach nonviolent conflict resolution one afternoon a week.

It isn't much, but at least it keeps me in touch with people whose lives I need to know about, prisoners. Most of the boys in my class were born unwanted, raised unloved, have lived in kill-or-be-killed neighborhoods, and have few memories of secure and happy moments in their lives. They have reading problems, impulse control problems, rage problems.

I have no illusions that I can teach them much about nonviolence. I keep reminding myself: go out to Oak Hill and just be kind to those kids, and you'll be doing plenty. Of course I don't walk in and tell the eight or nine kids with whom I sit together in a circle, "Here I am again, Mr. Kindness. Soak it up, children, and do evil no more." Instead, it's just going back week after week. I bring an essay to read—something by Martin Luther King, Jr., on forgiveness, or a few lines from Gandhi, perhaps a poem by Gwendolyn Brooks, an essay by Claude McKay—and get the kids to talk about it. On that level it is teaching humanities to people who have been treated inhumanely and, often enough, have treated others inhumanely.

In the first class I taught, in the summer of 1998, there were twenty-three boys in the room, all of them ordered to be there. Most were in foul moods, having been herded out of the cellblocks across the yard to the school, their card games and TV shows interrupted. I hadn't uttered more than a few syllables when a boy in the back row, both arms well tattooed and thick as a python's body, called out, "How's this course be helping me to get out of here?" "I can't say exactly," I answered, "but it could help to keep you from coming back."

Seconds later a boy in the far corner—wiry, small-framed, and intense—had a question: "Hey, Mister, are you a racist?" I tried to remember the last time I'd been asked that. While thinking, and not recalling, I heard a voice in the other back corner call out, "Why you taking so long to answer?" I said that was the first time I'd ever had that question. But no, I wasn't a racist.

I have to say, I did enjoy this give-and-take. Straight to the point. Frank. And relevant.

This fall I have a smaller group of seven. Twenty-three was unwieldy, even with a guard in the room. The boys are from 9B, a protective custody unit. I never ask anyone what he's in for. On the outside we don't meet someone and ask what kind of messes they've been in. Why on the inside? The youngest member of the class is eleven. He rarely sits still. He doesn't speak, he blurts. He can't look at a page for more than five seconds. He makes eye contact with someone and shouts out, "Why you looking at me, dumb nigger?"

Do I ask a guard to take him away? Or try to engage him so he'll gain a bit by being in the group? I've tried both, with few signs either way that he's the better for it.

On a trip to Knoxville to give a talk to a group of social workers, a teacher at a Tennessee youth prison told me that she, too, had an eleven-year-old black boy in her literacy class: "He's a sullen kid most of the time, but the other day he was cheery and talkative. I asked him why he was feeling so good. He told me that he just heard that his daddy had gotten out of prison, 'and that's why I'm happy.' Then he looks up at me and says, 'Weren't you happy, too, when your daddy got out of prison?' It's assumed—everyone's father goes to prison."

At Oak Hill it's much the same. Whenever the topic of fathers comes up, most will say that he's in or has been in prison. Few know where their fathers are now.

It isn't much better with female inmates and their mothers. Last year I taught in the girls' section of the prison. Most were raised by grandmothers.

One afternoon, a fifteen-year-old came running into the group. "I just had a call from my lawyer," she announced joyously. "He got the judge to release me in two weeks." I said congratulations, and asked what's the first thing she would be doing on going home.

"Gonna get drunk, " she said.

"Why that?" I asked.

"I'm an alcoholic. That's what alcoholics do. We get drunk."

"When did you start drinking?"

She thought a moment and said, "I guess when I was about eight . . . "

Astonished, I interrupted and said, "When you were eight years old?"

"Oh, no, when I was eight months old."

She told the story. Her mother, fourteen years old, overwhelmed by the demands of infant care, didn't know how to get her baby to go to sleep at night. But she had a girlfriend, an "experienced" mother at sixteen who did know: "Give the baby a bottle of apple juice and spike it with gin, and the baby will go off to sleep real quick."

She did, and the baby became an alcoholic in the crib.

The Washington Center

Thirty-two students, all of them with semester-long internships at federal agencies, public-interest groups, or congressional offices, show up at 5 P.M. for a three-hour weekly class. Their home colleges range from big-name to no-name schools: the Ivies, Little Ivies, and Poison Ivies. It makes no difference to me. On the subject of nonviolence, all are in the same state of unawareness. None has ever taken a peace-studies course.

I try to save the students some money by ordering the two course texts myself at a discounted price and carting them in on a dolly. Bookstore markup is avoided. After distributing *Solutions to Violence* and *All of One Peace: Essays in Nonviolence*, a few students open their checkbooks and ask, "How much?"

I reply, "You decide."

Jaws drop, eyebrows rise, eyes widen. There is disbelief. A minor hubbub erupts, threatening to turn major. It goes on for nearly a minute. After the confusion runs its course, and everyone stops talking to his or her neighbor, a student—from Vanderbilt—raises her hand and asks, "What if we don't know how much to pay?"

I don't offer much help. "You decide."

More talk, more confusion. Another of the perplexed—from Stonehill College—asks: "But what if I give you twenty dollars for the two books and someone else gives you forty?"

"That's their choice. They decided. Now you decide."

Another, from Texas Christian University: "What if we pay you nothing?"

"You decide."

One more, from Florida State: "You're the professor. It's your job to determine the price."

"You decide."

Clearly, none in the class had ever taken a course that granted this much pocketbook power. These, and all students, have been conditioned to pay whatever someone orders them to, herded like sheep around the academic marketplace with never a bleat of protest. Book sales to college students is a racket: profiteering off a captive market, with little accountability to buyers. The odds favor the colleges; they are full-time sellers with power over part-time buyers.

I let the class go at 7:45, to leave fifteen minutes for individual loose ends to be tied. Some students come up with checks. They range from twenty-three dollars to forty-five dollars. One hands me a note saying he wants to look through the books more thoroughly and will bring some money next week. Some say they'll pay at the end of the course.

I congratulate them all. They're deciding.

Stone Ridge Sacred Heart School for Girls, Bethesda, Maryland

At first it doesn't appear as if anything extraordinary is going on. Eighteen high school seniors are in the classroom, part of a consortium program involving five private schools in lower Montgomery County, one of the nation's wealthiest.

The schools are Stone Ridge, Holton-Arms, Holy Child, Landon, and St. Andrews.

A half-dozen electives are offered every year in the consortium, ranging from Mandarin to AP calculus. After speaking at a student assembly in 1998, I was invited by the headmaster at Landon, a boys' school, to teach my course on nonviolence. Last year the site was Landon. This year Stone Ridge, a Catholic girls' school run by the Sisters of the Sacred Heart.

I am in awe of the sixteen girls and two boys who signed up: they come in at 7:10 A.M., an hour before school opens. A few live in the Stone Ridge neighborhood across the street from the National Institutes of Health, but most need to be up by 6 A.M. to have time for the drive to school. Seeing them walk into class, I wonder, in deep admiration, about the large reserves of self-discipline they must be drawing on. Then, too, what motivates that self-discipline?

Plenty of high schools, public and private, have their small bands of go-getters, but these are mostly the extracurricular whizzes who belong to four clubs, play two varsity sports, and effortlessly rack up hundreds of community service hours—all of it *after* school.

To be an early riser at age seventeen or eighteen—only a few do it. To the question—Why is this group here at this hour?—my hunch is desire.

Some confirmation comes when I ask everyone to write answers to a list of questions I have—some benign probings that let me learn something about each student. One of the questions is, Why are you taking the course and what do want to get out of it?

These are among the written replies that come back the next morning:

I have always admired Gandhi, since the seventh grade. I believe that nonviolence is the most effective way to get what I want: a just world. I want to learn about the history of nonviolent action. There is a whole side of history/social studies which I have not been exposed to. This class will be my vehicle to take me out to the real world and how to confront injustice. I will hopefully take what I learn and bring it to my activist groups and we can be more productive. Most of all, I want to be inspired.

◆

I'm tired of learning about wars and violent revolutions and never learning the peaceful alternatives.

◆

All my life I have been taught that war is passion, that people who flee from the draft are cowards, that it is noble to fight for your country. I am interested to know the arguments from the other side.

◆

I am interested in contributing in some way to making a more peaceful society. I'm hoping to gain the skills and knowledge to do so. Also, I hope that we will have many active discussions and debates, which seem to be absent in most high school classes.

◆

I am taking this course because I am ashamed of humanity. We seem to be focused on the sole purpose of killing and destroying all that is great and beautiful, including ourselves. I hope that I can become a better person and make a difference in this world.

◆

On a superficial level, I signed up with the intention to improve my problem-solving skills, to learn to share my opinion more openly, and to improve my writing. On a deeper level, I'm here to gain a greater awareness about the world, to learn how I can help, and to further my own spirituality.

◆

*I'm taking this course to broaden my view of the
political spectrum. I hope to gain a more open mind
toward the political views of others. I tend to be ex-
tremely set in my ways, which are mostly conservative, and I hope that by taking this class I will be able
to fully comprehend the pacifist viewpoint.*

◆

*I need to learn more about the world I live in. I want to
have to think about my personal views and challenge
them.*

◆

*I am the type of person who believes that there is room
for self-improvement every day. For that reason, I don't
really have many firm convictions of where I stand on
issues. That is not to say that I am apathetic. I am not
well educated on the subject of nonviolence, but I love
learning new perspectives and views. I am taking this
course out of pure interest. And to be honest, I am
really sick of regular courses geared toward an AP
exam.*

I'm blessed to have these children with me for the coming
year. To the student sick of fake academic rigor, I say that
I'm weary too of that style of education and that my course
will steer as far away from it as possible. During the first
week of class I level with the kids. I tell them that grading,
testing, and homework are all but useless, and that all three
are forms of academic violence that will be de-emphasized
here.

That might have had them break-dancing in the aisles, or
on top of the desks for the more agile ones. But I urge them
not be fooled. "This will be the most difficult, the most chal-
lenging and possibly the most infuriating course you'll ever
take. Because it's desire-based, not fear-based, and the desire must come from within. The desire to push yourself,
because it leads to inner growth that can't be measured by

grades, tests, or homework. Only you can measure the honesty and intensity of your desire."

Grading, testing, and homework represent teaching by fear. Scare kids into learning. Score well on tests, goes the meritocratic message, and pathways to success widen. Do poorly, and they narrow. Kowtow to a teacher's demands for test preparation, no matter how rote the drilling, or spend hours writing irrelevant papers, and the slavishness will pay off. So it is claimed. And at the end of the course parents can ask, if they ask at all, not what was learned in the course but "What did you get on the final exam? What's your final grade?"

The illusion of excellence remains. The heavier a kid's book-crammed backpack on leaving school, the more the kid is learning. Fear-based learning works for a while—until the course ends, when test-givers and graders can no longer intimidate and the once-intimidated are paroled.

Schools are peopled by two kinds of teachers: those who want power over their students, and those who seek power with. The power-over set are mind-controllers who preach that academic excellence demands a high price, with payments coming in the form of academic suffering: tough tests, rigid grading standards, and heaps of homework. Teachers who seek power with also believe in excellence, but that it must come from self-demand, not teacher-demand.

I understand the riskiness of the power-with approach to education. Some kids will see my course as the ultimate gut course, a pure blow-off. That's fine. They are likely to be the ones who in conventional tests-grades-homework courses learn how to manipulate the system by obeying orders to perform but doing it with no heart. They have been conditioned to believe that successful performance in school assures successful achievement in life. But Walker Percy's line keeps intruding on this fantasy: You can make all A's and go out and flunk life. In twenty years I have seen enough 4.0s pass through my courses and ten or fifteen years later be living wildly messed-up lives to know the truth of that. And to know, too, that the kids who can make demands on themselves and give full effort to reading and writing about ideas and issues they care about end up as self-assured and self-giving adults. I teach not to help students become thinking people but to help them become thinking and caring people.

My main challenge at Stone Ridge is to help each girl and boy to relax. Some of them walk in carrying a forty-pound backpack crammed with physics books, math books, English books, history books. Forty pounds of books! All in the name of homework. Most of the girls weigh less than 120 pounds. They're hauling one-third of their body weight!

Then there's the other load of fall semester senior year: the mental one of stressing out over college admissions, of getting into the best college, of unwittingly becoming like the model student in the fable by Carol Rinzler in her book *Your Adolescent: An Owner's Manual:*

> *Little Kimberly asks her parents, "If they tell you in nursery school that you have to work hard so you'll do well in kindergarten, and if they tell you in kindergarten that you have to work hard so you'll do well in high school, and if they tell you to work hard in high school so you'll get into a good college, and assuming that they tell you in college that you have to work hard so you'll get into a good graduate school, what do they tell you in graduate school that you have to work hard for?" Kimberly's parents answer: "To get a good job so you can make enough money to send your children to a good nursery school."*

To help reduce the strain on their backs and their spirits, I make a promise to them: I will never start off a class with the grossest turn-off words ever uttered by a teacher, "Students, we have a lot of ground to cover today." I ask the class to do themselves, and me, a favor: when they hear teachers say that, stand up and tell them to go become the cross-country coach.

University of Maryland

On Monday afternoons from 12:20 to 3:00, in a seminar room in Anne Arundel Hall, eighteen students in the General Honors Program are ready to go. All were invited to be in the honors program based on their high school records. The course offerings range from the exotic—"The McDonaldization of Society," "The Cultural Significance of Astronomy"—to the basic, "The Writing Workshop." In the course description booklet of honors courses, mine is advertised with this note, among others: "Class discussions are expected, and dissent is welcomed. One skeptic enlivens the class more than a dozen passive agreers."

To get the discussion started, and rousingly so, I begin the class with a quiz—this being a gathering of intellectuals for whom acing quizzes is as easy as Tiger Woods making birdies. But it's a quiz with a difference. I open my wallet and pull out a one-hundred-dollar bill, announcing that whoever can identify the six people whose names I'm about to call out wins the one hundred dollars. They look at each other. Is this for real? Is the one-hundred-dollar bill real?

I begin the quiz. Who is Robert E. Lee? All hands shoot up: the general who led the Confederate side in the Civil War. Everyone is one for one. Who is Ulysses S. Grant? All hands rise: The general who led the Union side. Who is Norman Schwarzkopf? The general who won the Persian Gulf War. Everyone is three for three and looking good.

Who is Jeannette Rankin? No hands go up. Who is Dorothy Day? No one stirs. Who is Jody Williams? No one knows.

The class wit—a finance major, it turns out—asks if he is entitled to fifty dollars because he knew the first three.

Sorry, friend. The game is all six or nothing.

I've done this one-hundred-dollar-bill quiz hundreds of times, before students in classrooms, before students in large assemblies, and before large audiences of educators. No one's ever won the one hundred dollars. It's safe money. It's safe, too, that everyone will know the first three but not the last three. They know the peacebreakers but not the peacemakers. They know the men who want to solve conflicts by killing but not the women who believe in loving.

My honors students didn't need to have it explained. By the end of the course, I told them, you'll know all about Rankin, Day, and Williams. "Hey," calls out the class wit, still at it, "do we get the same quiz then?" Funny boy.

School Without Walls

Sometimes I wonder if this school wasn't named presciently: it may soon be without walls. The three-story building, which seems to be tilting a half-degree a year, goes back to the Grant administration. It's the oldest structure in the neighborhood, on G Street between 21st and 22nd. Five blocks east is the White House, five blocks west the Watergate apartments. Power one direction, money the other, and in between an impoverished public high school serving some two hundred students.

I have nine of them: three sophomores, three juniors, three seniors. Four blacks, five whites, five girls, four boys. Michael Henry, one of the seniors, who went with his Unitarian church group to the peace conference last year at The Hague, is taking the course for the second time. He is voracious about the literature of peace. To get him into class again—the rule from on high is that courses that are passed can't be repeated—we had to strategize a bit. I changed the name of the course from "Alternatives to Violence" to "Solutions to Violence." That was enough to fool the computers, plus the "papercrats." If a student has enthusiasm for a course, that should be enough. Michael, the only D.C. public high school student to be a finalist for a National Merit Scholarship, has it.

For some first-class sport, I announce a game. It's called red car, green car. In an earnest voice—always be earnest the first day of school—I ask the students to leave the room, walk down the hall and stairs and go out the front door. Stand there for ten minutes and count all the cars passing on G Street that are either red or green. Count them as accurately as possible. After ten minutes, come back and I'll have two questions.

Obediently, the nine march out. I look from the window. There they are, counting reds and greens. Two have notebooks. This is no moment for sloppy counting.

As they walk in, I overhear them comparing numbers. "Five green, seven red?" "No, four green, seven red." "You sure?" "Absolutely, I can count."

They quiet themselves, ready for question number one: "Didn't anyone think that was a bit stupid, standing there counting red cars and green cars?" "Yeah, I did," says one of the bright lights. "Me, too," adds another.

Question number two: "If you thought it was stupid, why'd you do it? Why'd you go in the first place? Why didn't you say 'No, I won't go'?"

As with my honors students at Maryland, the point isn't missed here either. Don't cooperate with abusive power. When it tells you to do something stupid, say no. When it tells you to believe that armies are effective, say no. When it tells you that competition improves character more than cooperation, say no. When it tells you that governments tell the truth, say no. When it tells you that violence brings about peace, say no.

A few years ago I had a perverse moment while giving a lecture at a Midwest university to an audience of graduate students in journalism. They were getting their master's degree, learning how to furrow their brows like Ted Koppel on Nightline. This school even offered a three-credit course on brow furrowing for the future Teds.

It was raining that day, a torrent. I asked the students to go count red cars and green cars—for twenty minutes. In the downpour. They did. They came back soaked and drenched. I told them that even sheep would have refused.

They weren't in much of a mood for my lecture. These are future members of the media. Small wonder that much of U.S. journalism is so suckered or snookered by power. Few dare to resist the seductions, few question the inanities that pass for political wisdom. They stand in the rain counting cars and come back in saying it means something.

October

> # Give the World
> # Your Best, Anyway

The purpose of education is to make the young as unlike their elders as possible.

—WOODROW WILSON

I will not raise my child to kill your child.

—BARBARA CHOO

University of Maryland

In political science, sociology, and government courses, professors routinely hail the wonders of democracy—giving the *demos* their say. Who could be against that? A few of my students are, at least the warier ones when I ask them to move beyond platitudes and express themselves democratically by voting in class on which topic they want to study next. The chapter in our text on Tolstoy? The one on King? Dorothy Day? I remind them that this is their school, their money, and their time, qualification enough to give them a voice in what they want to learn. Some students are uneasy. Does a "wrong vote" affect the final grade? Naturally they're nonplused. After years of being academically cowed, bossed, and herded—and paying for it all the while—suddenly they're actually being asked for their preferences on what they want to learn? What's the catch?

On assuring them there is none, I ask the class which chapter in *Solutions to Violence* we should read and be prepared to discuss this week. Four chapters are proposed: women and nonviolence, Tolstoy, Martin Luther King, and Dorothy Day. We vote. King wins.

"But which King?" I ask. "The safe, sanitized, mythologized, I-have-a-dream King that much of America, needing its illusion that racism is a thing of the ancient past, feels comfortable with? Or the uncompromising antiwar King who advised high school and college students in the mid-1960s not to fight in Vietnam, resist the draft, and, if needed, break the law?"

"That King," the class says. "You'll find him," I replied, "in his April 4, 1967, essay 'Declaration of Independence from the Vietnam War.'" No one had ever read it. Nor does anyone know that King gave his last Sunday sermon—also an antiwar speech—only ten miles from the Maryland campus, at the National Cathedral in Washington.

My students are part of an entire generation that has gone through schools whose texts ignore King the antiwar pacifist. In *Lies My Teacher Told Me: Everything Your American History Book Got Wrong,* James Loewen of the University of Vermont examined the twelve most commonly used high-school-level U.S. history textbooks. He reports that "King, the first major leader to come out against the Vietnam War, opposed it in his trademark cadences: 'We have destroyed Vietnam's two most treasured institutions—the family and the village. We have destroyed their land and their crops. We have corrupted their women and children and killed their men.'" No textbook quotes King on Vietnam, though all carry "I Have a Dream" excerpts.

In today's class discussion, students are unsettled—and two or three shocked—by King's line: "The greatest purveyor of violence in the world today [is] my own government." A debate breaks out. "That was the America of 1967," it is said, "not the America of 2000 when we are at peace and not at war with anyone. Look at the violence of Milosovec, or Saddam Hussein. Those are the bad guys." Someone counters with another quote from the King essay: "A nation that continues year after year to spend more money on military defense than on programs of social uplift is approaching spiritual doom."

No one expected the United States to be attacked by terrorists less than a year later. No one expected to be at war in a few short months.

To bring some context to the debate, I hand out a quiz, the Martin Luther King Memorial Exam, otherwise known as the "Quick Political Scholastic Aptitude Test" (QPSAT). I give fair warning: "If anyone flunks this test, I will be duty bound to put it on your transcript." Fidgeters fidget, squirmers squirm.

Quiz

As compiled and documented by historian William Blum, here is a list of the countries in which the United States military, funded by Congress, has been active since the end of World War II:

China 1945-46
Korea 1950-53
China 1950-53
Guatemala 1954
Indonesia 1958
Cuba 1959-60
Guatemala 1960
Congo 1964
Peru 1965
Laos 1964-73
Vietnam 1961-73
Cambodia 1969-70
Guatemala 1967-69
Grenada 1983
Libya 1986
El Salvador 1980

Nicaragua 1980
Panama 1989
Iraq 1991-99
Sudan 1998
Afghanistan 1998
Yugoslavia 1999

The quiz: In how many of these instances did a democratic government, respectful of human rights, occur as a direct result?

Choose one of the following:
  0
  zero
  none
  not a one
  a whole number between –l and +1

It's impossible to flunk. Everyone gets an A! And the list has grown longer since 1999.

The quiz is relevant also to King's line that we are called on to "go out into a sometimes hostile world declaring eternal hostility to poverty, racism, and militarism." All the nations that the United States attacked militarily were heavily populated by poor people, and most were people of color.

On the issue of military spending, I pass out the latest newsletter from Women Strike for Peace, one of my reliable sources for information that the corporate media rarely supply:

> *The Fiscal Year 2001 Defense Appropriations Bill Conference report was completed on July 17 for a total of $287.8 billion, a massive $21.7 billion increase—the largest since the Cold War—from last year's appropriation and $3.3 billion more than the White House request. Together with defense funds included in the Department of Energy and Military Construction bills, the total FY 2001 Pentagon funding for war adds up to $309 billion.*

Except for the math or astronomy majors in my class, the numbers are too immense for ordinary mortals to grasp. I break it down to manageable sums: $309 billion comes down to about $700 million a day—still beyond comprehension— or $8,000 a second. I ask if anyone in the class had a summer job that paid $8,000. No one did. $4,000? No one. $2,000? Four hands went up. "Congratulations," I call out. "You earned one-fourth of one second of the U.S. military budget. Congrats to me to, too: my payment to teach this course is $3,200, less than a half-second."

Another fact from the Women Strike for Peace newsletter brings it home: "We spend $13.7 billion a year ($52 for each taxpayer) in foreign aid to help the world and $309 billion ($1600 apiece in taxes) to fight it."

After two and one-half hours of reading and discussing, I think my students have a small, reliable inkling that the ideas of King—he died more than ten years before anyone in the class was born—are relevant to their current lives.

It's only an inkling, for sure. But that's enough for now. Inklings first, then leanings, then maybe bondings.

School Without Walls

At fifteen, sixteen, and seventeen, the ages of everyone in the class, teenagers are shopping around for ideals to live by. This week I was reading a bit of Mother Teresa, whose Sisters of Charity have three convents in Washington and whom I interviewed when she opened the last one in the southeast part of the city. I ask a student to read aloud a few of the nun's lines that might help everyone, me included, to keep on keeping the faith and sharing the peace, to be the idealists we are meant to be.

Anyway

People are unreasonable, illogical, and self-centered.
Love them anyway.

*If you do good, people may accuse you of
    selfish motives.
Do good anyway.
If you are successful, you may win false
    friends and true enemies.
Succeed anyway.
The good you do may be forgotten tomorrow.
Do good anyway.
Honesty and openness make you vulnerable.
Be honest and open anyway.
What you spend years building may be
    destroyed overnight.
Build anyway.
People who really want help may attack
    you if you help them.
Help them anyway.
Give the world the best you have and you
    may get hurt.
Give the world your best anyway.*

We discussed these ideas, with no concern from me where the talk would take us. The class appeared grateful to have a few moments to talk about ideals. Some wondered how much of their lives should be given over to helping others or to causes, when so much evidence stands there like a brick wall awaiting heads to hit against it. I offer a Mother Teresa story. A Western reporter, one who was far from convinced that the nun was as saintly as her admirers claimed—after all, she took money from Charles Keating, often visited Senator Jesse Helms in his office, and probably would go so far as to have a kind word for Zacchaeus, the tax collector—went to Calcutta to get the lowdown. Arriving at the hospice, he was told that Mother Teresa was busy attending to a dying beggar at the far end of the ward. After waiting a while, the reporter made his way to the mat holding the dying man. Mother Teresa, with a water basin and washcloth, was cleaning his body. The stench hit the reporter, as did the sight of the emaciated, sore-covered flesh of the man. Finally, he could take no more. He went close to the nun and said, "I wouldn't do that for all the money in the world." Mother Teresa looked up and said, "I wouldn't either."

Stone Ridge

Maybe I shouldn't notice, much less care, but the sight of heavy book-loaded backpacks the students carry in every morning keeps getting to me. A remedy exists: field trips. I worry that too many students, especially those from expensive private schools, have too many teachers stuffing ideas into their heads to stagnate there and be "unstuffed" onto the pages of the make-or-break final exam. And in that academic pudding will be proof, we're led to believe, that the kids have learned—or not learned.

The problem with idea- and theory-based education is that students become idea-rich but experience-poor. My solution is the school van: pile the kids in and go someplace for the day that may wake 'em up and shake 'em up. Not a field trip to still one more museum, play, or exhibit, but to prisons, homeless shelters, poor urban elementary schools where they can get close to some of the world's disaster areas and perhaps be stirred to get personally involved in offering solutions.

I arranged to take the Stone Ridge class to Garrison Elementary School in the morning and, five blocks away, the Luther Place Memorial Church women's shelter in the afternoon. Garrison, about a mile north of the White House, is in the Shaw neighborhood. Most of its 475 African-American students are on the free breakfast and lunch program, come from single-parent homes, and have few stable adult males in their lives. I have been taking my students to Garrison since 1990, after writing about the gritty efforts of an educational rarity: a black male kindergarten teacher. On the second floor was another: a black male fourth grade teacher. I asked them if I could bring in my students from time to time and have them tutor one-on-one some of the Garrison kids. Anytime, was the answer.

The other person with whom I work at Garrison is my son John. In 1992, after playing minor league ball for a year in the Baltimore Orioles organization, he began giving motivational talks to children in District of Columbia schools. One of the schools was Garrison. After an assembly he realized that few of the children had picked up on his references to baseball. It wasn't their sport. John asked the principal if he could organize a baseball team at the school. "You'd be welcome here," she said. He's been a volunteer coach ever since.

The first pick-up game on a bare, dirt, glass-strewn field behind the school was a revelation. In the first inning a fourth grader hit a grounder to short. He ran toward third base. He was thinking clockwise. When one team scored its first run, they called it a point.

After getting to know his players, as well as many of their teachers, John learned that reading problems were rampant at Garrison. Why teach kids how to hit and throw baseballs if they end up as illiterate adults? He founded Elementary Baseball, a non-profit literacy and sports program; making the team required coming to an after-school reading program. For tutors, he recruited his students at Wilson High, where he had begun teaching a course on nonviolence the year before. But the Garrison children needed mentors, too. By chance, John knew one of the judges at the D.C. Superior Court, a man who confessed that much of his work on the bench is sending young black males to prison. "Why not mentor kids before they mess up?" John asked the judge. Within a year, a half-dozen judges were mentoring at Garrison.

After eight years the reading abilities of the Elementary Baseball kids have been among the best in the school. No one runs to third base from home plate anymore. Word about the program's success spread. In 1998, ABC News wanted to send Sam Donaldson and a camera crew to tell the story. The plan of an ABC producer was to have John say a few words about the Garrison kids, with that being a lead-in for Colin Powell—then touring the land promoting his America's Promise program—to hold forth to Donaldson on the glories of volunteerism. John told ABC to get lost. No deal. The Garrison kids aren't to be used as props for Powell's self-serving image-making. If Powell cares about kids as much as he claims, John told ABC, have him go to Iraq and apologize to the families whose children were killed by the war Powell helped engineer and who have been dying since as a result of the economic sanctions. Undeterred, ABC found another school to serve as a backdrop for Donaldson and Powell to express their unction for the poor.

Others in the media—CNN, *USA Today*, *The Washington Post* and *Washington Times*—have come to Garrison to tell the Elementary Baseball story. Isn't it heartening, most of the reporters say, to see inner-city kids playing baseball and that here's a coach teaching them the skills that might get a few of them to the big leagues. As patiently as he can, and knowing well enough the innate obtuseness of the media, John explains that that's not the story. His goal is to use baseball as a way to get the Garrison kids involved in literacy and the values of education, not so they will have futures as big-league or minor-league ballplayers but futures as owners of big-league and minor-league teams. Enough black athletes are out there, but not enough black owners who are providing jobs for people. John tells his Garrison kids to become like Jackie Robinson the college graduate, Jackie Robinson for whom breaking the color barrier in baseball was one thing but breaking it in the business world was another. That's why Robinson didn't become a coach or manager after the Brooklyn Dodgers. He put on a business suit and tried to penetrate corporate America, where the real power—economic power—is.

Only one of my Stone Ridge students had ever been in this part of Washington. Years back, on a field trip to Garrison, one of my seniors at Bethesda–Chevy Chase High School told me that she didn't like going into the ghetto. It might be the other way around, I suggested. You're in a ghetto—Chevy Chase—and maybe it's time to look beyond it.

"Take a chance and come on the field trip," I said. She did. After meeting the Garrison children and spending a day with them in the classroom, the stereotypes—about poor people, blacks, the "dangerous inner city"—fell away. Soon after, she became a regular tutor at the school. At college she threw herself into service learning programs.

At Garrison this week we arrive at 8:45 A.M. The principal, an African-American woman in her mid-forties and a former classroom teacher, gives us a welcoming talk. She has a list of rooms for my students to go into, with teachers awaiting them.

When taking classes on field trips, I follow up by inviting them to write about what they learned, in addition to sending thank-you letters to their host teachers. One of the Stone Ridge girls, Michelle Dellatorre, wrote a reflective essay that is—despite the ordinary opening lines—laced with self-analysis not common to high school seniors. It reads:

> The field trip to Garrison Elementary was a good time. The fun I had stands out in my mind more than anything else. Working with the children made me feel useful, appreciated, and like a kid myself. But these children were far from childish. They were intelligent, accepting and inquisitive, qualities seldom found in adults or my peers. I was extremely impressed.
>
> Though they possessed so many great qualities, I was particularly touched by their acceptance of me. I must admit that when we set out on the field trip I was concerned that in a nearly all African-American school, where there aren't many Caucasian teachers, that, putting it simply, the children or teachers might not like me. I know that in elementary school, I was in an almost completely white Catholic atmosphere. One boy, Rold, was African American. Although I probably talked to him more than the other boys, he was a boy, and I was deadly shy, and so my contact with anyone of the opposite sex and anyone of non-Caucasian background was extremely limited.
>
> I can't remember knowing any African-American girls my age until I came to Stone Ridge, and Stone

Ridge itself is far from being a very diverse community. Though I now have African-American friends, it took me awhile to form these friendships. This is mainly due to my being somewhat ashamed of being Caucasian. Frankly, the history of my race is pretty horrid. The countless suppressions of rights and human dignity that my race has been responsible for, until recently, and even in the present day, are disgusting, and if I were not a member of the suppressing race I think I might be rather bitter toward all of its members.

Even if I am not responsible for the crimes against humanity and prejudices that are held by members of my race, it is still a nasty family history to be born into. It is because of this history that I always feel extra cautious when approaching people of other races. I feel they have the perfect right to be less accepting of me, and that I have to try extra hard to break down this barrier of distrust. This perception is, for the most part, constructed wholly in my head. My friends do not feel this way toward me, nor do many of the African-American people I met, but I still somehow feel the need to apologize for my race. When my friends talk about racial issues, I feel ashamed that I am one of, though by color only, the perpetrators of evil in this world. Needless to say, all of this is a constant source of trouble and questioning for me.

That is why the acceptance that I received at Garrison Elementary was so valuable. Coming from my background and my thought processes, the gift of being able to walk into a classroom and make friends with everyone, with no questions asked and no issue made of anyone's race, was such a joy to me.

Those kids liked me for who I am and not what color I was. It was more important that I could joke with them than whether or not I had shared the same heritage or grown up in the same neighborhood. Knowing that I was capable of making those children's day better despite the fact that I wasn't exactly like them made me

*feel so happy, and wholly brightened my outlook on
people and the world in general.*

*The field trip was such a positive experience. I am so
glad that we had the opportunity to go over there and
meet all those incredible people. Although I have only
touched on one aspect of what made the excursion so
meaningful, I know that it must be clear that there
were many other as important and as enriching facets
of the experience. I can't thank you enough for arrang-
ing this trip.*

*I hope that it continues to be an important part of
future classes.*

I'm hoping, too. High school administrators tend to see
field trips as larks, fine for grade school kiddies but unpro-
ductive after that. Keep teenagers, especially seniors and
juniors who need to be prepped for college, cooped up in
fact- and idea-driven classrooms, especially the AP classrooms that will get them into the Princetons and Stanfords,
there to have a well-programmed and studious roommate.
Too often, we process students as if they were slabs of
cheese—going to Velveeta High, on their way to Cheddar U
and Parmesan Grad School.

It would help if schools gave credit for service learning.
Tutor at a grade school while taking a sociology course, and
write a paper comparing the experience with what Jonathan
Kozol wrote in *Savage Inequalities*. Or help in a homeless
shelter and read *Tally's Corner* at the same time. Or volunteer in a congressional office and read Rep. Andy Jacobs's
political memoir, *Slander and Sweet Judgment*. Then ideas
in a book are matched to realities in life.

Serving food to homeless people in a shelter a mile from
the U.S. Capitol is useful, but it can remain idle charity unless accompanied by an awareness of policies inside the
Capitol that keep money flowing to build weapons, not af-
fordable housing. Learn which political structures underlie
the nation's persistent poverty and guarantee what the definition of politics truly is: who decides where the money goes.

Oak Hill

Six boys pull their chairs around. Four more would be here, but they are locked in their cells for the rest of the day following a fight—not a chair-throwing melee, I'm told, but still a slugfest for a few minutes. "Just a one-rounder," jokes one of the boys.

I bring three of my students from Walls, all girls curious about prisons and the people in them. I make it a point to introduce everyone, the same as would be done on the outside. One of the Walls girls has a Philippine background; her dark skin makes her appear African American. One of the Oak Hill boys says he knows her.

The girl asks where did they meet.

"At a friend's party."

"Which friend?"

"Not sure."

"Which party?"

"Not sure."

The other boys tell him to quit lying. He says he's not.

They say he is, that he does it all the time. They tell the girls to ignore him.

He grabs his crotch. "You know what you can do with this."

Before Round Two begins, I interrupt. "Time for the Kind Word Exercise," I announce, "now that the Mean Word Exercise has gone so well."

It's done like this. Sitting in our circle, I say a kind word about the person to my right, he says one about the person to his right, he says one about the person to his right, and around the circle.

At Oak Hill this almost always lowers the tension. Few kind or gentle words are ever exchanged in the daily grind of confinement. Many of the inmates maintain their swagger, either as a self-defense tactic or to send the message that they were once neighborhood powers in their street days.

I get the circle going: "Ronald has a strong voice and is a good reader." A faint smile crosses his face. He looks to his right, at Dwayne, a muscular eighteen-year-old a few months into his third stretch at Oak Hill: "Dwayne, he knows how to take care of himself. And he's a nice guy." Dwayne turns to Jason. He doesn't say anything. Five seconds pass. Ten seconds. Then, "Jason, he's religious. He reads the Bible."

The Kind Word Exercise takes no more than five minutes. To make sure that everyone knows why we do this, I pass around "Loving Your Enemies," the sermon Martin Luther King, Jr., delivered at the Dexter Avenue Baptist Church in Montgomery, Alabama, on Christmas Day, 1957. I ask Ronald, the good reader, to read aloud the fifth paragraph:

> There is some good in the worst of us and some evil in the best of us. When we discover this, we are less prone to hate our enemies. When we look beneath the surface, beneath the impulsive evil deed, we see within our enemy-neighbor a measure of goodness and know that the viciousness and evilness of his acts are not quite representative of all that he is. We see him in a new light. We recognize that his hate grows out of fear, pride, ignorance, prejudice, and misunderstanding, but in spite of this, we know God's image is ineffably etched in his being. Then we love our enemies by realizing that they are not totally bad and that they are not beyond the reach of God's redemptive love.

We read the rest of the essay aloud. Some boys decline to read. Others asked to be called on and then read falteringly, stumbling over any word with more than two syllables. The discussion is about who has needed, and who has given, forgiveness. One boy, sixteen, sitting backward in his chair, says he doesn't believe in forgiving anyone. "Make people pay for hurting you." Two others agree. Stories are told about neighborhood gun battles. "You think I should forgive a punk who tried to kill me?" a boy asks.

"Yes," I answer, moving the group back to King's essay where he argues that forgiveness is not only a theological virtue but a practical skill; it lets you leave behind the garbage of the last fight. Otherwise you keep hauling it around, never free of it. One boy agrees with King's view. "I've forgiven people. It's helped me."

On leaving, the boys crowd around the Walls girls: "You coming back?"

"You like us to?"

"You crazy? Come back tomorrow."

Georgetown Law

Out of sixteen students, only three have heard of Dorothy Day. Of those three, only one can cite the name of any of her books.

"All of you have a strong case," I announce, "backed by sixteen years of hard evidence, for an educational malpractice suit. Sue your past schools for willful negligence. They didn't teach you about the life and ideas of one of the twentieth century's boldest radicals for peace. Ask for both compensatory and punitive damages. Go for millions! And any loot that comes in goes toward funding what's really needed at Georgetown Law, the Dorothy Day Chair for Lawbreaking."

I get a few quizzical looks. What was that all about? Is he serious?

For class I had asked everyone to read the chapter with Dorothy Day's essays, including "Love Is the Measure," "Poverty and Precarity," "This Money Is Not Ours," "From Undeclared War to Declared War," and "Reflections in Jail."

These are among my favorites, ones that I go back to when my spirit needs to be fired up. They remind me of the first time I met Dorothy, in 1962, when I was living with the Trappists at Holy Spirit Monastery, Conyers, Georgia. The abbot invited her to speak to the community on a Sunday afternoon. One of the priests, Father Charles, had run a Catholic Worker House of Hospitality in Cleveland before joining the Trappists. Through him, everyone in the community knew that Dorothy was as close as mortally possible to living Christ's gospel. She served and lived with the poor, practiced the works of

mercy and rescue by running her own House of Hospitality—she disdained the term *homeless shelter*—on the Lower
East Side of New York, and encouraged people like Jack
English—later to be Father Charles—to open their own houses
around the country. In 2000, more than eighty-five are in
operation, three of them in Washington.

As expected, Dorothy spoke to the Trappist priests and
lay brothers about the origins of the Catholic Worker in the
early 1930s after her conversion from a life of mild hedo-
nism to Christianity—early pre-Augustine Christianity in
which nonviolence and communistic sharing of wealth were
taken seriously.

Dorothy's talk was proceeding smoothly, with the shaved
heads of many monks nodding in pious agreement. Then
she unloaded. Paraphrasing, I remember her startling message as this: Don't get too carried away, good fathers and
brothers, with your Trappist image. Don't buy into the world's
opinion of you, that you are the holiest of the holy just because you rise at 2 A.M., sleep in unheated dorms, eat no
meat, fish, or eggs, are cloistered, speak with sign language,
do manual labor on your farm, are cut off from your families.
In many ways you are living with a kind of security to be
envied. Your needs for food, clothing, and shelter are guar-
anteed. When sick, you get free health care at the Catholic
hospital in Atlanta. You have a well-stocked library, your meals
are farm fresh, you have ample time to pray and meditate, no
kids, teenagers, or panhandlers are around to bother you, and
when you die you get a high requiem mass, a free burial plot,
and a sure pass into heaven. You call that a hard life?

I went to Dorothy's funeral in late November 1980 at Na-
tivity Catholic Church on the edge of the Bowery and a half-
block away from Mary house, where she had lived. More than
eight hundred people followed the pine coffin to the church.
The day before, the secretary of the cardinal of New York—
the Most Reverend Terence Cooke—had phoned the Catholic Worker House to request that the funeral Mass be held at
10 A.M. because it would then fit into the cardinal's schedule
and he could preside. But Dorothy Day's daughter Tamar

had already decided on 11 A.M. That was when the soup kitchen closed for the morning break between cleaning up after breakfast and getting ready for lunch. The cardinal's presence would be missed, the secretary was told, but with all due respect, feeding the hungry came first.

None of the nation's 285 Catholic bishops thought enough of Dorothy to be in the church that morning. A Protestant bishop was there—Paul Moore, a friend of Dorothy's and a spiritual ally. Lately, talk is heard from the Catholic hierarchy that Dorothy ought to be put up for canonization. The effort brings to mind the two-line verse written by an Athenian poet about the sudden shift in opinion on Homer once the trouble-maker was safely departed:

> *Seven Grecian cities begged for Homer*
> *dead,*
> *Through which the living Homer had*
> *begged his bread.*

To bring Dorothy Day's commitment to pacifism and social justice alive, and to move beyond what might be only feelings of edification produced by reading her essays, I bring Arthur Laffin to class. He is as close as anyone I know to carrying on Dorothy's work. Forty-five years old, he has lived for the past ten years at the Dorothy Day Catholic Worker House in Northeast Washington, a three-story home on a residential block where refugee families are taken in. One day a week Arthur takes the community's donated van to restaurants, bakeries, and other outlets to pick up unsold food otherwise headed for dumpsters. He runs a meal line across from the White House for the city's poor. For years every Monday at 7 A.M. he and other Catholic Worker members protest at the Pentagon, praying at the River Entrance as thousands of war planners file in. On Fridays at noon he and other pacifists picket the White House in protest of the economic sanctions against Iraq. He and others regularly picket the Israeli Embassy on behalf of Mordecai Vanunu, imprisoned by Israel for eighteen years for revealing that his government had nuclear weapons. He has made two trips to Iraq to visit hospitals and offer comfort to families of children who are dying because of the sanctions. Over the years he has been arrested more than seventy times on charges of civil disobedience—he calls it, correctly, civil resistance—at U.S. military bases, nuclear weapons silos, the headquarters of military contractors, and congressional buildings. He has served time on a half-dozen convictions in federal, state, and city jails.

Arthur Laffin is not, how to put this, the typical guest speaker at Georgetown Law. Whether out of curiosity, awe, or amazement, my students are receptive. They take to him. Arthur, who played professional basketball after college, is 6'4", trim and angular. His voice is husky. He speaks unhurriedly and to this class, and all the others I have invited him into, says nothing remotely preachy or judgmental. He has a taste for irony and for the occasional wry note, as when he says that the toughest hardline judges he has faced are Catholics.

He tells the law students that the state sees him as a chronic lawbreaker. "That's fitting," he smiles, "because that's how I view U.S. policymakers, breakers of such laws as the War Powers Clause of the Constitution—Article One, Section Eight—the Geneva Protocol, Article 54, which prohibits 'starvation of civilians as a method of warfare,' and the Executive Order forbidding conspiracy to assassinate. All of that involves U.S. policy toward Iraq."

To put himself into context Arthur reminds the students that only a few months before Roman Catholic Bishop Thomas Gumbleton of Detroit called President Clinton and other administration officials war criminals for imposing economic sanctions on the people of Iraq. He also referred to Denis Halliday, the chief humanitarian worker for the United Nations in Baghdad, who resigned in protest in late 1998 and said that the "sanctions are starving to death six thousand Iraqi infants every month, ignoring the human rights of ordinary Iraqis and turning a whole generation against the West."

Arthur brings photographs to class from his last visit to Iraq. He and a group of Americans organized by Voice in the Wilderness, a Chicago pacifist community, spent ten days in cities and villages to see and hear in close, personal ways the suffering that is, for most Americans, a distant abstraction. "Not once in my time there," he says, "did I experience any hostility because I was an American. Instead, I was treated with kindness and generosity. In the hospitals I saw children dying and suffering from diseases they would never have had without the sanctions. I can remember the children's names: Khafar, Zahra, Ann. These are kids that officials in the Clinton administration treat as expendable, all in the name of getting at the demonized Saddam Hussein, the former honored friend and weapons client of the United States."

In Iraq, Arthur went to the Al Ameriyah shelter where more than eleven hundred Iraqi civilians were bombed and burned to death by U.S pilots in 1991. On this trip and an earlier one Arthur brought medicine and medical supplies to give to Iraqi doctors and nurses. "That was another of my criminal deeds," he smiles. "The U.S. Treasury's Office of Foreign Assets Control says it's a crime to violate the sanctions. We've been fined $163,000."

I bring to class *Swords and Plowshares: Nonviolent Direct Action for Disarmament, Peace, and Social Justice*, the 1996 book that Arthur co-edited and which I use as a resource. I pass out his essay *Reflections on a Lenten Fast and Public Witness,* which has these lines written on the thirty-eighth day of a diet of only water and juice:

> *As the fast draws to a close, I am more keenly aware of the preciousness of life as well as the victims of greed in our world. During these moments when I crave a sumptuous meal, I think of what it must be like for the more than 35,000 children who die daily from hunger or preventable diseases. While I know I can eat in a few days, these sisters and brothers cannot. God have mercy on me and on our world for allowing this scandal of hunger.*

Students have questions. About his years of antiwar protests, arrests, and jailing, they ask, "Do you think you're getting anywhere?"

"That's not for me to decide," he answers, "and what does 'where' mean? Success isn't something I think about. I go with the idea that we aren't called to be successful, we're called to be faithful."

"What about all the laws you've been breaking," another asks. "Should citizens be allowed to pick and choose which ones they want to obey or break?"

"That's a matter for conscience," he answers, "and the trick is—the obligation is—to work hard to have an informed conscience. I believe that laws represent the failure of love."

The last thought is uttered so softly that I fear many students may have missed it. If they ever hear a line closer to the truth, or more basic to human relationships, or more needed in a country where laws routinely sanction the violence of executions, bombing civilians in enemy nations, and selling of weapons to dictators, I can't imagine what it would be.

By the time they're in law school, students have well-developed noses for sniffing out frauds, especially pretenders ever ready to dispense their Washington wisdom to the untutored. In Arthur Laffin the class might have had the least phony, and the most authentic, speaker ever to come before them. Midway in his talk he spoke of his opposition to the death penalty. Nothing exceptional about that; he's a pacifist, so of course he's against capital punishment. But then he startled the class: "A year ago my brother Paul, whom I loved deeply, was murdered. It happened on a sidewalk outside a soup kitchen in Hartford, where he volunteered. The person identified as Paul's killer was a mentally ill man whose illness had gone untreated. I've been praying for him this past year. At Paul's funeral mass, our family asked that the attacker be forgiven and be provided the psychiatric help he needs."

Arthur brought to class some copies of *The Little Way*, the monthly Catholic Worker newspaper published out of Dorothy Day House. He edits and writes for the newspaper. It's

only eight pages, but it carries news not found elsewhere—
the news of resistance, of conscience, of faith, of mercy.

Students take copies. On leaving class they thank Arthur
for coming. Some thank him, as I do, profusely.

The Washington Center

Without a grounding in Gandhi, a course on nonviolence
won't amount to much. "What does anyone know about
Gandhi?" I ask. A few students tell me they saw the 1984
movie. It won an Oscar, they remember. One student says
he took a course last year in international relations in which
the professor said that Gandhi's ideas were fine for India in
the 1930s and 1940s but would never work anywhere else.
Try Gandhian tactics with a Hitler.

I am tempted to take on that question—it comes up every
semester—but I want to save it for later, after the class has
read some essays on the Danish resistance to Hitler and excerpts from Philip Hallie's *Lest Innocent Blood Be Shed*—the
story of Le Chambon and the French villagers who hid Jews
in the early 1940s and used weapons of the spirit to defy the
Nazis.

For class we read Gandhi's "My Faith in Nonviolence" and
"Doctrine of the Sword"; "Ahimsa" by Eknath Easwaran; and
"Gandhi in the Postmodern Age" by Sanford Krolick and Betty
Cannon. These are but a passing taste of Gandhian thought.
A full semester could be devoted to his ideas and still not get
that deep into them. Gandhi wrote five hundred words a day
for all his adult life, the whole body collected in ninety-five
books. Ten years ago I had a student at Maryland—Jim Otis—
who took to Gandhi like few others I've ever taught. "An ocean
of Gandhi's writing is there," I said offhandedly to Jim after
class one day. "If you ever have time, dive in."

A decade passed before I heard from Jim again. He phoned
one day to say that he did indeed find time to read Gandhi
and would like to send a gift by way of thanks for my sug-
gestion. "It would be most welcome," I said, thinking the gift

would be a photo of Gandhi at his spinning wheel or a memento of some minor kind.

The next day a Fed Ex truck pulled up to my house to unload fifteen boxes of some heft. Inside were the collected works of Gandhi, all ninety-five books, sent by Jim Otis with a breezy note inviting me to take up a bit of diving. Jim, living in Beverly Hills and married to Linda Henson, another Maryland student whose father, Jim, also went to Maryland, is a writer and filmmaker currently at work on a documentary about history's enduring practitioners of nonviolence. Four years ago Jim wrote a piece for *The New York Times* Sunday magazine on how, like Gandhi, he sets aside one day a week for total silence, not speaking to anyone.

In reading through the collected works, not many books pass before three Gandhis emerge, the spiritual, the political, and the strategizing Gandhi. For this week's class I'm teaching the practical Gandhi, the one whose ideas on nonviolent conflict resolution are usable in dealing with both life's minor daily irks and the inevitable major cataclysms. By definition, conflict means only this: we need to change our way of dealing with one another, because the old way isn't working. Whether it's across a living room or across an ocean, conflicts will be faced either through violent force or nonviolent force. No third way exists. Anyone who says, "I like to avoid conflict," should be given a one-way ticket to Mars, Neptune, or Pluto. On earth, what Whitehead called a third-rate planet revolving around a second-rate sun, we have conflict. Almost always it's a signal to get another way of dealing with disagreement, from roommates to earthmates. Judging from the history of our wars, our bents toward genocide and homicide, spouse and child abuse, abortions, the killing of animals for food, death-row executions, it's as if the art of resolving conflicts nonviolently was as incomprehensively difficult to learn as astrophysics in Urdu.

Based on Gandhi's teachings, and as interpreted by Dudley Weeks and other Gandhians, these are the nine steps of decreasing or ending violence.

• *Define the conflict.* The one place cops most fear to be sent is to a home or apartment where a domestic dispute is raging. A drug bust or high-speed chase is minor compared to the risks of calming a husband-wife battle. Family therapists report that in as many as 75 percent of husband-wife fights, the combatants are battling over different issues. The husband is enraged by what his wife said or did today. The wife is out of control over what her husband said or did three weeks ago. They can't settle their conflict because they don't know what it's about. It's this to him, that to her.

The dynamic of battling over differently defined issues was on display during the buildup of the Persian Gulf War. Iraqi President Saddam Hussein and President George Bush, leaders of two governments long accustomed to solving conflicts by killing people, defined their dispute differently. For Hussein, it was a property issue. Land under Kuwait's control really belonged to Iraq. Bush defined it several ways. First it was oil. Then it was jobs for Americans. Then it was the old standby: America must stop naked aggression—as against, presumably, clothed aggression.

Here were two politicians, as self-righteous and self-deluded as a warring husband and wife, unwilling to find a common definition of the conflict.

Defining clarifies. When you clarify, you see. When you see, you can deal.

• *It's not you against me, it's you and me against the problem.* The problem is the problem. Most people, and most nations, go into battle convinced I'm right, you're wrong. I'm good, you're evil. I'm smart, you're stupid. I deserve to win, you deserve to lose. Even if one side does win, the first reaction of the loser is, I want a rematch. I'll come back with meaner words, harder fists, and bigger bombs. Then you'll learn, then you'll behave, and then, after cleaning up the blood, we'll have peace forever.

Few can give up this illusion. But by focusing on the problem, and not the persons who have the problem, a climate of cooperation, not competition, is enhanced.

♦ *List the relationship's many shared concerns*, not the one unshared separation. What concerns? The daily ones of family life: enough food, clothing, and shelter, enough emotional support. These are the strengths of the relationship. They remain. If the strengths—the shared concerns—are given more attention than the lone unshared separation, chances for reconciliation increase. In Ernest Hemingway's *A Farewell to Arms,* the most soulful of his novels, as against the chest-thumpers, a character is described in a pure line: "He was strong in the broken places." If a relationship is strong in the broken place, it is likely to mend.

♦ *When people have fought, don't ask what happened.* The question is irrelevant. They will answer with their version of what happened, almost always self-justifying. The better question is, "What did you do?" This elicits facts, not opinions. Misperceptions are clarified, not prolonged. Skilled trial lawyers, whether in civil or criminal cases, don't ask people on the stand what happened. Instead, they ask, "What did you do?" Juries are instructed, or should be, to decide on the relevance of factual information.

♦ *Active listening is better than passive hearing.* Listening well is an act of caring. Talented listeners have many friends. Poor listeners have many acquaintances. A television commercial showed a self-consumed CEO barking from behind his oversized desk, "When I talk, people listen." The enlightened way, the reconciling way, is to turn that around: "When I listen, people talk."

The main thought in my mind on entering a classroom is, listen well to your students. First off in the semester, the kids want to know if their teacher is a listener or one more know-it-all gasbag.

♦ *Choose a neutral place to resolve the conflict, not the battlefield itself.* Armies sign peace treaties far from the war zones. Too many emotions are there. In some schools around the country where progressive faculties are teaching, peace rooms are in place. Anyone who was fighting—in the schoolyard, the halls, the buses—automatically knows to go to the peace room at a set time, say Friday morning from 9:00 A.M. to noon. Who will be there? Mediators: classmates who have been trained in the essentials of Gandhian nonviolent conflict resolution. Principals and counselors in schools that have peace rooms see the results in lower rates of violence.

+ *Start with what's doable.* Restoration of peace can't be done quickly. If it took a long time for the dispute to erupt, it will take time to end it. Work on one small doable, like getting home on time rather than being habitually late. Almost always, it's a laughably small wound that causes the first hurt in the relationship. Divorces rarely happen from high dramas—a husband running off with Madonna to frolic in the Greek islands, or a wife leaving everything to go photograph bridges in Iowa with Clint Eastwood. It's never that grand. It's always prosaic, like a husband who keeps criticizing his wife because she puts too much salt in the soup or a wife who harps that the husband never takes the kids off her hands. Correcting that is doable.

+ *Increase forgiveness skills, decrease vengeance urges.* Many seemingly large-minded people are willing to say after the conflict, "I'm going to bury the hatchet." To themselves, they add, "But I'm going to mark exactly were I buried it, just in case I need to dig it up for the next war."

Forgiveness looks forward; vengeance looks backward. It's why we have eyes in the front of our heads, not the back. Forgiveness means leaving the garbage of the last fight behind. Otherwise, we let our emotions become trash haulers. Settling scores never settles conflicts.

+ *Purify our hearts.* This is merely an elegant way of telling yourself, "I need to get my own messy life in order before I tell others how to live." Jim Douglass says, "The first things to be disrupted by our commitment to nonviolence will not be the system but our own lives."

Gandhi believed in self-purification. A story is told of a mother who walked from a distant village to visit Gandhi in his ashram. She brought her little boy. "He won't stop eating sugar," she told Gandhi. "It's bad for his health but he won't listen. But he'll listen to you, Gandhi, you're his hero. Please tell him to stop." Gandhi looked at the boy, pondered, and told the mother to come back in one week. Slightly irritated— it was mid-summer and the village was far away—she left. The next week she came back with her child. Gandhi patted him on the head and told him to stop eating sugar, that it's bad for one's health. The mother thanked Gandhi profusely. Walking to the gate of the ashram, she turned to ask Gandhi why he didn't say that the week before. "Mother, until one week ago I was eating sugar!"

Before letting the class go, I asked how many have had conflicts with their roommates. Only six weeks into the se- mester, two-thirds of the hands went up. The disputes were the usual: leaving the bathroom a mess, ignoring unwashed dishes, bringing friends into the room at 2 A.M., not turning off the phone at night, and on and on.

Sending them off, I suggested it was time to become Gandhians, apply the nine steps, and start to lurch toward peace.

For a laugh—and it's a wasted class without two or three good ones—I offer advice to the women and men in the class. If someone phones you for a date, tell them, sure, you'll go out with them, but on one condition. That they know the nine steps of Gandhian conflict resolution! If they say no, hang up. With that standard, you probably won't have much of a social life. But you'll be safe.

And it works the other way. Next time you're in a singles' bar looking for love, walk up to a prospect and say, "Hey there, good looking. Guess what? I know the nine steps of Gandhian conflict resolution." It's the greatest pick-up line ever uttered!

November

Ideas to Practice,
Not Mull

One should seek out an audience that matters. In teaching, it is the students. They should not be seen merely as an audience but as a part of a community of common concern in which one hopes to participate constructively. We should be speaking not to but with. That is second nature to any good teacher, and it should be to any writer and intellectual as well. A good teacher knows that the best way to help students learn is to allow them to find the truth by themselves. Students don't learn by a mere transfer of knowledge, consumed through rote memorization and later regurgitated. True learning comes about through the discovery of truth, not through the imposition of an official truth. That never leads to the development of independent and critical thought. It is the obligation of any teacher to help students discover the truth and not to suppress information and insights that may be embarrassing to the wealthy and powerful people who create, design and make policies about schools.

—NOAM CHOMSKY

Stone Ridge

Nearly every moral, social, or political issue I ask my students to read about and then discuss in class and reflect on in papers tends to remain only that, an issue. War planning, though it goes on daily ten miles away at the Pentagon and three miles away at the nation's largest weapons company—Lockheed Martin in Bethesda—is an abstraction. Students can think and talk about it, but after that, what can they do? The same for the death penalty; they think and talk, read, take a position, but that's it.

It's time now for an issue that isn't an abstraction, one that demands personal decisions and choices every day: nonviolence toward animals.

But how to teach it? Come on too strong—refer to meat as dead, rotting, chemicalized animal body parts—and you are dismissed as a fanatic. Come on as an intellectualizing theorist gabbing about the rights of animals, and you are one more academic bore.

Another problem. How far do I take students? Is reading enough? We'll go through "The Ethics of Nonviolent Eating" by Helen Nearing, "The Animal Rights Position" by Tom Regan, "Respect for Animals" by Isaac Bashevis Singer, "Blue" by Alice Walker, *A Vegetarian Sourcebook* by Keith Akers, "Animals My Brethren" by Edgar Kuper-Kobertwitz, and "Animal Rights and the Law" by William Kunstler. What about films? I have at least a dozen, gathered over two decades and ranging from an HBO documentary, "To Love or to Kill?" to a ten-minute PETA exposé—"Meet Your Meat"—that graphically but realistically shows how pigs, cattle, and chickens are caged and slaughtered by food-company workers.

Every high school class I've taught has had girls and boys who have made commitments, with varying intensity, to live without exploiting or killing animals, directly or indirectly. It's helpful to get them talking. On this subject students will listen to each other with more openness than they will to me.

When I ask who, if anyone, has had a conversion to animals rights, a third of the hands go up. Ten years ago it would have been one or two students, if that. Some give up flesh-eating for ethical reasons, some for health, and others for environmental protection, and a few for a mix of all three.

I call on Victoria Paal, a Holton-Arms senior who often wears a Compassion Over Killing tee shirt. She belongs to the group, founded five years ago by Paul Shapiro, one of my former students and now a senior at George Washington University, who designed his own peace-studies major. Its members regularly picket McDonald's, Neiman Marcus, and other companies that earn profits off the bodies and hides of animals. Victoria, a politically aware Green Party supporter who reads newspapers to stay informed, tells the class of her conversion. Sophisticated, she sticks to her personal narrative without making any judgments about people who eat meat or wear leather. She is aware that critics of the animal-rights movement look for any reason to portray its members as self-righteous zealots ready to rap those who have meat-based diets as morally inferior. I'm relieved that she stays clear of that line. This is no stone-thrower letting everyone have it from the largest glass house in town.

When I ask the class if anyone subscribes to *Animals' Agenda* magazine, Victoria is the only one. "I just wrote an article for it," she says. Much praise to you, I tell her. Get your ideas into print. Two days later my copy of the November/December issue of *Animals' Agenda* came, with Victoria's five-hundred-word reflective essay on page 32. It also carried a photograph, a wide-smiling girl, with her blond hair slung back, who is crouched over the front end of a full-grown seven-hundred-pound Yorkshire hog. Victoria volunteers at an animal sanctuary that gives a home to rescued mammals, primates, and fowl. In the photograph Victoria's right arm is caressing the nape of the hog who, on coming to the sanctuary, had the happy fortune not to be one of the 21 million factory-farm animals slaughtered that day for America's table.

I'm as elated as can be, proud too, when one of my students gets published, whatever the viewpoint expressed. Five years ago a senior boy in my class at Bethesda–Chevy Chase High wrote a letter to the editor at *The Washington Post* knocking a column I had written criticizing Magic Johnson for being a full-time athlete but a part-time father. The student, a fan of Johnson, had challenged my thinking in class, but I said do more than just vent at me. Take time, exert some effort, and send your views to the paper. He did. I brought the article into class and had it read aloud, with me leading the applause when it was done. I take more delight in one student who disagrees with me and puts energy into expressing it than a roomful of students who agree passively.

But back to Victoria. This is her essay:

It was a bad day for a vegan in the school cafeteria. The lunch options included egg noodles, meatballs, or soggy peas soaking in lukewarm water. I moved to the salad bar but the dressings had cheese or honey in them. I settled for some lettuce.

At my high school, I am aware of two other vegans, both in the senior class with me. I have been vegan for about three years. When I first decided to go vegetarian five years ago, I knew very little about it. Something just seemed wrong about eating an animal. After all, I would never eat my dog. Two years later, after reading about veganism on web sites, I decided it was a good option for me. At that point, I was not very concerned with my health or the environment. I simply felt that it was wrong that dairy cows and hens were killed prematurely and kept on factory farms.

I will never forget the day I told my parents. "Vegan? What's that?" my mom asked. After I explained it, she rolled her eyes. My parents' worst nightmare was to have a liberal daughter. She continued, "It will be too hard. You won't get enough nutrients. It's not a good idea." My dad sat across the table, laughing, and swallowing a mouthful of steak.

Even after discussing the topic, my parents remained adamant that it would be a bad idea. My mother was panicking that I would not be getting three glasses of milk a day. I explained that there were other sources of vitamins and minerals, and my parents eventually realized that this was a decision from which I was not going to back down.

Now, more than three years later, my mom still likes to think it's a typical adolescent phase. When I say I'm not going to eat something because it has whey in it, I know to expect her to roll her eyes. My father still forgets occasionally and will offer me fish at dinner. At the same time, however, they seem to have grown used to my lifestyle. My mom gets excited when she finds a new vegan ice cream, and my father loves trying to find good vegan food at restaurants. They are even beginning to learn what vegan and nonvegan ingredients are.

I, too, have learned a lot over time. But reading such books as Diet for a New America, I better understand the implications of a meat-based society on human health and the environment. I have also become more socially active and aware. Through working with such animal rights groups as Compassion Over Killing, I have been given the opportunity to participate in protest and rallies. I was also fortunate enough to find a great part-time job at a vegan store near my home.

My school is gradually becoming aware of students' lifestyle choices. When it came time for the rat dissection in biology class, students were offered the alternative of participating in a computer-based interactive virtual dissection of the human body. However, when I took up this offer I was not spared from several teachers' disapproving looks and lectures on how I would learn more by actually dissecting.

Each day is a bit of a battle for a high school vegan. While the familiar arguments and occasional lettuce lunches can get aggravating, veganism is a choice that pays off in the end. I am able to feel better about myself as a person, knowing that I am doing a small part to protect the animals.

I copy the essay and pass it around the class. What a schoolmate writes has immediacy. During the next few weeks we will go through the readings, watch the HBO and PETA films, and give everyone a chance to have a say. As in all our discussions and debates, I remind everyone that we may not always see eye to eye but we can always talk heart to heart.

I make it a point to give everyone the option of leaving the room during the films. Scenes of legalized gore can upset the sensibilities of students raised in a flesh-eating culture in which the annual advertising budget for McDonalds is $800 million, where the taking of animals' lives in slaughterhouses is seldom reported in depth either by the print or electronic media, where newspapers routinely run sports section "outdoors" columns about the joys of killing animals and fish, where religion is used to justify violence done to animals— the dominion lines in Genesis 1:28—and where those who work to live in harmony with animals are either called on to defend their odd ways or are dismissed as dreamers or fanatics.

I savor these three or four weeks of teaching animal rights. Often it is only a line or two from an essay that gets a class discussion going. These are sure starters:

The animals of the world exist for their own reasons. They were made not for humans any more than black people were made for whites, or women created for men. (Alice Walker)

♦

I am in favor of animal rights as well as human rights. That is the way of a whole human being. (Abraham Lincoln)

♦

I cannot help thinking that our exploitation of animals has a direct link to our exploitation of our perennial human victims: African-Americans, poor whites,

Latinos, women, lesbians and gays, social activists, Native Americans, and Asians, to name a few dis- empowered groups. (William Kunstler)

♦

The word "vegetarian" derives from the Latin "vege- tus"—whole, sound, fresh, lively. The meat humans eat is neither whole, sound, fresh, or lively. It is dislimbed, tainted, decaying, stale, and dead. A diet consisting of green leafy vegetables, root crops, grains, berries, nuts, and fruits supplies all the body needs for strength and well being. (Helen Nearing)

♦

I have no doubt that it is a part of the destiny of the human race, in its gradual improvement, to leave off eating animals, as surely as the savage tribes let off eating each other. He shall be regarded as a benefactor of his race who shall teach man to confine himself to a more innocent and wholesome diet. (Henry David Thoreau)

When I hear from students ten, fifteen, or twenty years after they leave school and my class, sometimes I ask what they remember about this course. Often it's the section on animal rights. The ideas, they say, were ones to be prac- ticed, not merely mulled. The refrain "I haven't eaten meat since the class" is common. One student from years back said the one line she most remembers is, "If it has a mother, don't eat it." Another recalled the time a guest speaker— from the Center for Science in the Public Interest—displayed a test tube three-quarters filled with five ounces of caked animal fat, saying that this was the equivalent of a Big Mac, a large milk shake, and an order of french fries. The tube of gunk explains why the leading cause of death in America is heart disease. Fruits and vegetables aren't causing coronar- ies.

The Washington Center

Eight weeks into the course, the first of two fifteen-hundred-word papers is due. Before collecting them, I ask the students if they are capable of being totally truthful. The question puzzles them. "Of course," they answer. "All right, take a moment and write on the top right-hand margin of your paper, first, the amount of effort you put into the paper—if 100 percent effort, write 100 percent; if 85 percent, 85; if 60 percent, 60; if no effort, 0 percent; whatever. And second, is this the best paper you ever wrote, yes or no. If you can't be honest about this," I say, "no problem. Just write 'Sorry, I can't be honest.' At least you'll be honest about that."

People glance at each other with those *what's-this-all-about?* looks students flash when the unexpected drops into their ordered lives. They tell me that no teacher had ever made this request. I reply that I do it all the time, on the perhaps eccentric notion that brains are what you're given, effort is what you give back.

I collect the papers. Out of thirty-two, only two have 100 percent on the right top. The rest range from 98 percent and 93.7 percent—obviously a math major, that one—down to 73, 65, and 40 percent. Two carry a yes, the 100 percent effort papers. The rest were noes.

I take the papers home and in the next week read them, starting with the two 100 percents. Crisp language prevails, along with reasoned arguments, factually based opinions, and ample references to researched material. The sub-100 percent papers run deep with cliches, linked together like Polish sausages and about as deadly. Several papers have a dashed off last night feel. A few look to be recycled, crops rotated from a sociology course last year. After ten papers, my chronic illness flares up: MEGO, My Eyes Glaze Over.

On returning the papers the next week, I announce that while each essay has been read, only the 100 percent and best-ever papers received my comments and evaluation. The rest nothing. I resist saying that they should be grateful I even brought them back. Why be a trash hauler?

Hold it, someone calls out. He says he was honest when putting down "85 percent" and "no." I have to resist again and not say, "What do you want, sir, a medal or a chest to put it on?" Others pile on. They, too, were totally truthful. Doesn't that count? Sure—and now I can't resist—it counts about as much as keeping your eyes open during class and breathing. You're *supposed* to be honest; it should be automatic.

Another ten minutes pass. We had other papers to write, they protest. Internships take up our time. My roommate is noisy. How can we improve if we don't get feedback? The consensus is that 98 percent is good enough, 90 percent is good enough, 40 percent is good enough.

I'm not buying. Good enough never is. This is ice-water time, a splashing on top of them of my chilling view that writing is too sacred a craft to be trifled with and, second, the deepest joy in life is found in wholehearted exertion. For those who remain unpersuaded—the majority—I offer a final thought. "After college, when you are job hunting, do you plan to tell your employer that you will be giving 80 percent effort? Do you ask your sweetheart for a date and say you'll be only 70 percent attentive, or 40 percent? For those who played a varsity sport back home, how many times did you tell the coach you'd be giving 80 percent effort during the big game?"

Whether in my class or anywhere else, those who aren't self-demanding and self-disciplined won't be self-made. Motivation needs to come from within. Schools have a raft of artificial inducements to stir students' minds, ranging from the usual cowings of tests and homework to fear mongering: if you want to "get ahead" in life, work hard and make A's. These failed non-solutions imprison everyone, just as prison guards are only slightly freer than inmates. They also prop a school's agenda by leaving teachers in control of learning, as if learning is meant to stop at the close of the semester or graduation. Quality teachers see students as combustibles. Set them on fire with a passion for useful knowledge and they will burn for a lifetime.

How to rouse students to be self-demanding is the mystery of teaching. Jeff Spoden, in the history classroom for sixteen years in the Mt. Diablo, California, school district, is the editor of *To Honor a Teacher*, a 228-page collection of essays and poems by former students about their most influential teachers and coaches. In none of the essays—by bus drivers, social workers, poets, educators, politicians—is a teacher or coach remembered for tough grading policies or killer final exams. One writer tells of being "a scholastic drifter" in high school, one who "lacked collegiate ambition." Another "hated school" and had been a "screw-off in high school." One was a "misguided teenager and lost soul amid six hundred other students." All might have remained that way, except for a caring teacher. Spoden writes:

> While grades do have some relevance, using them to assess meaningful learning is like looking at a paint job to determine the structural integrity of a house. Learning is profound when a passionate teacher creates a challenging environment in which students explore powerful ideas. There is no significant place in the equation for a bureaucrat sitting in an office deciding precisely what every student in a state should know.

Schools dispense enormous amounts of irrelevant information and, often enough, the hired spreaders of it—pension-waiting teachers who have given up—stay on and on. They are uncomfortable knowing their students as people, as if individuality could lead to a loss of classroom control. As it surely does. But an uncontrolled classroom is where the deepest learning—the kind that leads from ideas to action—can happen. How can imagination be controlled? Or the unconscious? It is the caroms and bounces of life experiences that shape a philosophy.

Before self-discipline can occur—turning in the best paper ever with 100 percent effort behind it—a sense of the self needs to be nurtured. If it leads to a touch of classroom disorder, the loss is minor compared with the gain—the chance for a teacher to be at the place where a student's natural intelligence converges with inner effort to produce a thing of value.

University of Maryland

After initial uneasiness the class now likes to be polled on what topic should be next. "It's your money, your time, and your future," I tell them. "What interests you most?" Trained to be passive, students are accustomed to professors laying out the course plan the first day with a detailed class-by-class schedule, like a cross-country train that has arrival and departure times down to the minute. But what if students—intellectual travelers who are the paying customers—aren't in a hurry and prefer to linger on an idea, the better to savor and absorb it?

I prefer to teach that way. I won't be hired by Amtrak anytime soon. My train isn't for the speed driven.

This week a majority votes to examine the death penalty. Now is an ideal time for it. This fall news stories on the death penalty are cascading onto the public consciousness. In Virginia, there is the running account of Earl Washington, Jr., fourteen years on death row and finally cleared by DNA. In Illinois a Republican governor calls for a moratorium on executions after the *Chicago Tribune* tells of thirteen death-row prisoners being freed for reasons of innocence or lack of evidence. In Texas absolutist claims are made that every last one of the 150 executions overseen by Governor George W. Bush was mistake free, while elsewhere since 1977 eighty-eight people—victims of mistakes—have walked off death row exonerated. In Washington, bills in the both the Senate and House propose a number of safeguards to prevent more blundering.

To limber minds, and to get into the subject in a participatory way, I pass out my Death Penalty Trivia Quiz, a true-false exercise.

1. Of the thirty-eight death penalty states, thirteen, including Texas and Virginia, allow executions of mentally retarded people.
2. Five methods of killing are used in one state or another: gassing, hanging, drugging, shooting, and electrocuting.
3. The electric chair in South Carolina is called Old Sparky, as was the chair in Florida.
4. The Association of Government Attorneys in Capital Litigation, which strongly favors executions, is known as the Fryers Club.
5. In 1992 Governor Bill Clinton flew to Arkansas during the New Hampshire primary for the execution of a brain-damaged man whose last meal included a piece of pie as dessert. On leaving his cell to be lethally injected, he told a guard that he didn't eat the pie because he wanted to save it for after the execution.
6. The 1996 Anti-Terrorism and Effective Death Penalty Act makes it more difficult for prisoners to obtain federal review of claims that their constitutional rights have been violated.
7. St. Thomas Aquinas, among other Roman Catholic saints, was an ardent supporter of the death penalty.
8. Louisiana executed a black teenager whose body was so small that two phone books were put under him so his head could reach the electric chair cap.
9. At a southern execution, the prisoner's last words were, "I'm about to learn a lesson."
10. In 1997 in Florida, after a man's head caught fire while he was being electrocuted, State Attorney General Bob Butterworth said, "People who wish to commit murder, they better not do it in the state of Florida because we may have a problem with our electric chair."

11. Prison guards on death row are told to watch out for suicidal inmates, to keep them from killing themselves before their executions. More than forty-five death-row inmates have killed themselves since 1973.

12. At a recent execution the prisoner asked to be allowed to take his bible with him to the electric chair. His request was denied because the bible might catch fire.

13. In the early 1980s the warden of California's San Quentin prison placed a newspaper ad saying that anyone wishing to witness an execution should phone to reserve a seat. The switchboard was swamped with calls. Fifty requests were granted. Any higher number would create a fire hazard, ruled the fire marshal.

14. In 1981 the French minister of justice, Robert Badinter, ended capital punishment in France. He gave one of the country's two guillotines to the national museum in Paris. The second was sold at an auction. The buyer was a Texas millionaire who put it in his game room.

15. When a six-year-old shot and killed a classmate in Michigan, the *Sun,* a British newspaper, speculated that American ingenuity would come up with a solution: build a kiddie-size electric chair.

16. Senator Orrin Hatch of Utah, in 2000 the Republican chair of the Judiciary Committee, said, "Capital punishment is our society's recognition of the sanctity of human life."

17. While governor of California, Ronald Reagan favored lethal injection as the ideal means of killing condemned prisoners. He said that's how horses on his ranch were put down. "The horse goes to sleep. That's it."

18. The Texas death row holds several men whose lawyers fell asleep during their trials. In October 2000 the U.S Court of Appeals for the Fifth Circuit denied the appeal of a man whose lawyer slept. The court cited a Supreme Court finding that the prisoner must prove that his lawyer's napping affected the trial.

19. In September 1988 a California newspaper reported that Vice President George Bush received "wild applause"

from high school students for stating that he strongly believed in the death penalty.

20. A 1995 Hart Research poll of U.S. police chiefs found that the majority do not believe that the death penalty is an effective law-enforcement tool.

21. The day before Velma Barfield was executed in North Carolina, Billy Graham phoned her: "Velma, you're going to beat us home. Tomorrow night you'll be in the arms of Jesus."

22. Seven members of Pennsylvania Abolitionists United Against the Death Penalty were arrested in October 1997 outside Philadelphia's Criminal Justice Center for distributing informational fliers. The charges included "obstructing the application of justice through picketing." One of the fliers was titled, "How Racism Riddles the U.S. Death Penalty."

23. A September 2000 Justice Department report stated that nearly 80 percent of federal prisoners are members of minorities. They account for 74 percent of the cases in which federal prosecutors seek the death penalty.

24. In 1994 Congress expanded the number of crimes eligible for capital punishment to more than forty.

25. Eighty-two percent of those put to death since 1987 were convicted of murdering a white person, even though people of color are the victims in more than half of all homicides.

26. Since 1976 the South has had 80 percent of the nation's executions and the highest murder rate of any region.

27. A Duke University study found that the cost of executing a person in North Carolina was $2.1 million. If applied nationally to all executions, the cost of the death penalty since 1976 exceeds $1 billion.

28. At least 381 homicide convictions have been overturned since 1963 because prosecutors concealed evidence of innocence or presented evidence they knew was false.

29. Over 90 percent of those tried on capital charges had court-appointed lawyers. Not one state meets the American

Bar Association's standard for the appointment of counsel for poor people.

30. When the Texas Senate passed a bill to overturn a law that allowed executions of profoundly retarded people, and the House was about to concur, Gov. George Bush stopped further action by saying, "I like the law the way it is right now."

31. Three hours before his scheduled execution in Texas, Johnny Paul Penry, whose IQ is below 60, was told by the warden that the Supreme Court gave him a stay. The warden—accompanied by the chaplain—came to the cell to read aloud the court's wording. Of the warden, Penry said: "He couldn't read it to me, so he gave it to Father Walsh to read. The warden didn't understand the Catholic language, and it was in Catholic. Father Walsh read it to me because he understands Catholic."

I give the class about twenty minutes to mark their trues and falses. Conversations erupt. Students ask each other if this or that one really could be true. Some statements cause muffled laughter: Billy Graham's farewell to Velma Barfield, the Fryers Club, the guillotine imported from France to a Texas game room, the Arkansas pie story.

Only a few students mark all thirty-one true. A student from a Catholic family says the one about Thomas Aquinas must be false. Not only is it true, but it was only recently that the Vatican came out against capital punishment in all cases. Gradually, a consensus emerges that each is true.

"Almost," I say. "There's a curve ball. One is false." That starts a guessing game. After a minute, I tell them. "Number eight, the black teenager with two phone books under him? It wasn't Louisiana. It was South Carolina. Stay on your toes next time, I'm tricky!"

Without an occasional laugh, the insanity of homicide sanctioned by the state would be unbearable.

After years of classes on the death penalty, I've found that most students have strong views either for or against but little awareness of the actual laws, politics, or procedures that oil the gears of the death machine. The subject is part of the course because the problem of what to do with people who kill is solved, as with all other social problems, either with violent or nonviolent solutions.

Despite what it's called, the Death Penalty Trivia Quiz is a jolt to most students. The piling on of well-documented facts causes astonishment or bewilderment in some, disgust in others, and, for a few, anger. But those favoring the death penalty tend to stand firm, arguing that however flawed the process is, the idea remains sound: The state does have a moral right to exact retribution. Don't do away with executions, just eliminate the inefficiency.

To keep the class debate from being overly cerebral, I invite a friend who has, to understate it, a bit more than a casual or academic knowledge of the death penalty. He is Joseph Brown, an African American who spent thirteen years on Florida's death row before being released in 1987. Calling himself Shabaka Sundiata Waqlimi—Swahili for uncompromising teacher of truth—he lives in Washington, is married, and works at the Father McKenna Center. At 5'10" he is muscular, with thick forearms. I know him from the Father McKenna Center, a food, counseling, and job-training program housed in the basement of St. Aloysius Church, a Jesuit parish a few blocks east of the U.S. Capitol.

When introducing Shabaka to the students, I don't recall them ever being as rapt. They look intently, this surely being a first for each of them. Here is a person who would be dead if the state of Florida had had its way. He had come within thirteen hours of the electric chair.

In 1974 Shabaka received a death sentence following a capital conviction. A summary of the case by the Northwestern University Legal Clinic, which staged a national conference November 13-15, 1998, on wrongful death penalty convictions, states:

> Mr. Brown was sentenced to death after having been convicted of a murder, rape, and robbery. The evidence against him was the testimony of one Ronald Floyd, a

man who held a grudge against Mr. Brown because Mr. Brown had previously turned him in to the police on an unrelated crime. At trial, Floyd emphatically denied that there was any deal for his testimony and the prosecution repeatedly emphasized to the jury that Floyd had no deal. Several months after trial, Floyd admitted that he had lied at trial, and that he had testified in return for not being prosecuted himself for the murder, and for a light sentence on another crime. Nevertheless, the state courts granted no relief to Mr. Brown, whose conviction was ultimately reversed on federal habeas corpus. The prosecution declined to retry Mr. Brown, who was released.

Shabaka begins with a story about what was scheduled to be his last day on earth. He was moved from the main death-row cellblock to a cell closer to the electric chair, a standard ritual meant to calm the inmate and focus him on what was at hand. The day before the execution, the prison tailor came by to measure Brown for his death suit—waist, arms, and legs. Shabaka recalls that he pushed the tailor away and refused to cooperate, not only because he insisted on his innocence but because he felt demeaned by the tawdriness of the measurement gambit. What difference does it make if the suit is too small or too big?

The story stays in my mind. I've interviewed dozens of men on death row, many of them guilty of the most loathsome, unspeakable crimes. Most of the nation's annual twenty-two thousand murders involve alcohol consumption or drug use, are poorly planned, and are panic related. Some may exist, but I've never known or heard of a person convicted of capital murder who killed with the cold-bloodedness of the state: locking people in a cage day after day, month after month, year after year, and conveying daily the message that one day they will be taken away to be killed. The mental torture of that ordeal is not found in any homicides, save those in government death rows.

When a student asks Shabaka how he endured thirteen years of captivity with everything pointing to an electrocuted end, he told of being befriended by a young public-interest lawyer who believed in his innocence. He took the case with no experience in death-penalty law and, in fact, favored the death penalty. "But when he saw it up close," Shabaka says, "he had second thoughts. He spent $40,000 of his own money defending me. That doesn't include the $400,000 in other legal costs covered by his law firm." The attorney, Richard Blumenthal, is now the attorney general of Connecticut. A Democrat, he would have been chosen by the party to run for the Senate had Joseph Lieberman yielded his seat in the fall of 2000 when running for the vice-presidency.

Shabaka lost eleven appeals, including two denials for a hearing by the Supreme Court. At one point he was offered a deal: admit guilt for second degree murder and be released for time served. He said no, that he was innocent. "During my time on Florida's death row," he says, "sixteen men were electrocuted. Nine committed suicide. I myself thought about it. Many men lost their minds. The isolation is total. We communicated by yelling through walls. We had two hours a week for recreation. Two showers a week, for six minutes. Phone calls were forbidden, except to lawyers. I stayed sane by reading. The book that helped the most was *Man's Search for Meaning* by Viktor Frankl. Another was *The Souls of Black Folk*. My brother died while I was on death row. He could have been saved with a liver transplant. Mine matched, but I wasn't allowed to donate. I hold the state responsible for the death of my brother."

A student asked Shabaka about his life now. "I work with drug addicts and homeless people at the Father McKenna Center. It's run by the Jesuits, good men who take their religion seriously. I've seen poor people turn their lives around No human being is ever lost. I would love to say that I am at peace in my own life, but I'm not. I still have bitterness and resentment. I'm human. I was violated. I always knew the justice system was violent, racist, and unfair. Of course I'm angry. Who wouldn't be? But I control those emotions, but I don't mind telling you about them."

Shabaka reminds me of Paul Hill, one of Ireland's Guilford Four whose story was told in the film *In the Name of the Father*. Hill spoke to one of my classes in the mid-1990s, shortly after being released from fifteen years in British prisons for a crime he didn't commit. Students were amazed at how well he controlled his emotions.

I ask Shabaka whether Florida compensated him for his years on death row. No, he says, but he has a lawyer who is suing the state for a judgment of several million dollars.

Oddly, the idea of compensatory damages is rarely mentioned in the growing literature of wrongful convictions. Yet it should be automatic, a fund made available to the freed on the day they walk out of hell.

One of the inmates on Florida's death row with Shabaka was Willie Darden. I ask if he knew Willie. "Very well, all thirteen years I was there."

The week before, I had discussed the Darden case with the class, including his prison essay in "The Inhumane Way of Death," a part of *Solutions to Violence*. Darden, black and North Carolina born, had had six dates set for his execution, each one receiving a stay by judges, twice within twenty-four hours. His case—he was convicted in 1974 on a charge of killing Carl Turman in a furniture store robbery in Lakeland—came before the Supreme Court in 1986. By then groups like Amnesty International and members of Congress such as the House Judiciary Committee's John Conyers of Michigan had investigated the facts and were aligned with the movement to free Darden. Post-conviction evidence revealed that Darden was not physically present at the time of the slaying but was miles away. The two eyewitnesses to that fact were not called to testify at the trial.

One of those swayed was Justice Harry Blackmun. The Supreme Court ruled 5-4 against Darden. Blackmun dissented, writing that the opinion "reveals a Court willing to tolerate not only imperfection but a level of fairness and reliability so low it should make conscientious prosecutors cringe."

Blackmun went further. In a speech to judges in July 1986, in which he called the just-completed term "the most difficult of the sixteen years" he was on the court, he said: "If ever a man received an unfair trial, Darden did. . . . He got a runaround in that courtroom." Blackmun cited the prosecutor's summation to the jury in which he vehemently expressed a wish to see Darden "sitting here with no face, blown away by a shotgun." He was an "animal who should only be allowed out of his cell on a leash." For Blackmun, these and other statements violated Darden's right to a fair trial because they were "a relentless and single-minded attempt to inflame the jury."

On January 19, 1988, I wrote to Willie Darden offering my support. He knew of it already after someone had sent him a column I wrote on January 3 about the case. I invited him to come speak to my classes should he be freed: "I am fully confident you will be. If not, and they do kill you, be assured that I will tell my students about you and your case. Either way you will be an inspiration. If you have time and would like to write a letter to my students—with your thoughts on your life, your years in prison, and what you think of American justice—I would be happy and honored to have it and would bring it to class. Many, many people in this country, and around the world, are united with you. Don't feel that you are alone. Your struggle is everyone's struggle, your freedom our freedom. We are all working together. Bless you always."

On February 4, the day after the Supreme Court halted at the last hour Darden's execution and agreed to hear his appeal, Willie wrote back. The two-page handwritten letter was in calligraphy, inked ornately and with care.

> *My Brother,*
> *There have been only a few times in my life when*
> *I've been at a loss for words with which to express my*

*deepest of feelings. . . . Receiving your warmhearted,
spirit-raising letter has certainly presented me one of
those times.*

*With strong support from you and many others from
every corner of the world, Victory No. 6 [the most
recent stay] was won, and I am trying to unwind and
bring myself out of the storm and intensify my struggle
for justice and freedom. I have no time to relax from the
intensity my struggle creates within me.*

*Brother Colman, to speak to your students should
the bells of freedom tone loudly for me would be a
great honor. I will share with them all the terrible
experiences and inhumane suffering I have been
subjected to.*

*I have spent the last fourteen years of my life in
turmoil which, to me, has been nothing short of living/
existing in the worst kind of hell one human could
possibly introduce to another. When I think of America
the word "justice" does not come to mind. I cannot
associate the word "justice" with any part of America
because I've never received anything from America
that was representative of j-u-s-t-i-c-e.*

*I love America but hate that which she so violently
and inhumanely represents. Injustice and racism in our
so-called land of the free and home of the brave is
apparent, and lurks behind the doors of every branch
of government and every "law and order" agency in
America. I say no more!*

> *Much to you in the way of love,*
> *Brother Willie*

The next month, on March 15, with the Supreme Court 5-
4 against him, Darden was killed in the electric chair. Every
semester since, including this one, I bring Darden's letter to
class, have it read aloud and passed around, and suggest to
the students, if they are inclined, to remember Willie in their
prayers. I bring also an extended interview with Darden by

Amnesty International on February 11, 1988, which ran in *The Crime of Punishment*. In their preface to the interview the Amnesty authors wrote: "The case against [Darden] was at best circumstantial. There were questionable eyewitness identifications and a gun . . . that could not conclusively be tied to the crime." Helen Turman, widow of the victim, "picked out Darden as the killer [at an informal gathering]. Darden was the only black man in the room. A key actor in the story, who was never called at the trial, Rev. Samuel Sparks—the Turmans' minister—stated to an ABC television reporter that Mrs. Turman had told him, 'All blacks look alike to me, but the lawyers say he did it and that's good enough for me.' . . . Darden's witnesses were never called, although Christine Bass drove every day to the courthouse. She was ready to testify that Darden's presence in her front yard [at the time of the murder] meant he could not have been at the scene of the crime. As with so many defendants on public aid, his court-appointed lawyer failed him at every turn, and once during the trial even referred to his client as a 'nigger.'"

Yes, Shabaka remembers Willie Darden. So do I.

When class ends, students crowd around to thank Shabaka for coming. He has touched them, both by his account of fighting for his life and by his work among homeless men at the Father McKenna Center. One of the two black students in the class—a sophomore from a private school in Brook-lyn—wrote her reflections: "This was one of the best classes I ever had. I told everyone about it. It's important to speak with someone like Shabaka, who went through injustices like capital punishment. It was amazing to see how he is so willing to help people. He made me reevaluate what I do with my time and made me think about things I never did before."

Georgetown Law

After a class on Dorothy Day, Gandhi, and another on King, someone asks if we will get to Tolstoy. The questioner is Kevin

Allen, a third-year student in his late twenties whose path to law school is like no other I've known.

From a rural eastern Colorado town set in wheat fields, at sixteen he was selected by the American Legion to be a delegate to Boy's Nation in Washington, there to be greeted by President Ronald Reagan. "I was honored to meet a man who seemed to promote the ideals of democracy and liberty that my community valued," Kevin wrote in a paper for class. Two years later he turned down scholarships to several colleges to accept an appointment to the U.S. military academy at West Point, N.Y. "I would be a soldier." What he imagined West Point to be—its cadets "glorious and glamorous," their mission "true and just," could not be found on the day in late June 1988 that he reported for orientation. "I was whisked into a world of chaos and violence unofficially known as 'beast barracks.' I expected the shouting, the physical punishment, the psychological gamesmanship. What I did not expect, however, was the immediate, constant, and gratuitous emphasis on rape, human mutilation, and death. I will never forget the horror I felt as I stood in a dark hall, watching video images of killing while fourteen hundred other recruits, heads freshly shaved and wearing gray, shouted 'kill kill, kill' to the beat of hard-rock music. I was trained to be a killer. Soon I would be capable of ripping the enemy's heart out of his chest and eating it because I was ordered to do so."

Kevin survived his plebe year. That summer he began reading authors such as Noam Chomsky, Gabriel Kolko, and Eduardo Galeano, who linked the U.S. military—Kevin Allen's military—with dictatorships, torture, and mass violence. That fall he left West Point. "I could no longer live a life that contradicted everything good and pure in my heart."

His Colorado town did not bring out a brass band to greet him on coming back. He was labeled a quitter, a failure. "The high hopes for the hometown boy had been misplaced. 'We knew he would never make it. No one from these parts ever does.'" At nineteen, with no money and little emotional support, and needing to confront his feelings of failure, he joined a local Marine Corps reserve unit. He liked the $458 monthly check, plus the promised training as an air traffic controller. It meant one weekend a month and two weeks a summer. No direct combat was involved.

In the fall of 1990 Kevin enrolled at the University of Colorado at Boulder. He took courses in Gandhian philosophy, black politics, and Latin American history. He discovered Tolstoy. "Here was a great writer, a former soldier, arguing that patriotism was not a good, but a deplorable evil that pitted one state against another, dividing and killing people."

With the Persian Gulf War revving up, the Marine Corps ordered Kevin to active duty. He debated with himself on whether to refuse the orders on ground of conscientious objection or to follow them. He took the second course, reluctantly, and put in four months of active duty. "Wracked with the guilt of reporting for war," he wrote, "I determined that I would make amends for my sins through a life of public service. On returning to Boulder, I took courses in peace studies, economic development, religion, and philosophy. I started volunteering for social justice organizations and cultivated friendships with activists in the peace community."

After graduation Kevin joined the Peace Corps. He served in the Dominican Republic, working with subsistence farmers and agricultural cooperatives. Fluent in Spanish, he followed his Peace Corps service with work in Bogota, Colombia, researching human rights abuses. After more studies—in international human rights law at the University of Chile—he came to Georgetown Law.

I have had students before who were in the Marine Corps or in the Peace Corps, but never one who had been in both. Law students like Kevin Allen, who have been out of the classroom a few years—kicking around after undergraduate life, getting out of the United States to see a bit of the world, paying rent, taking a few bumps, figuring out what their gifts really are—are annealed by those realities, toughened into a maturity not usually found in those coming straight from college. Many of the latter are 4.0 brainiacs, with high LSATs and confident that intellectual power—which carried them this far, after all—is all that matters in life. They have a passion for success but not often a passion for service.

The Kevin Allens come to law school with specific experiential knowledge of one or two social problems and ready to acquire the skills needed to help solve them. When I had the class fill out a questionnaire—Benign Queries—the first week, Kevin wrote that his main interest was "international human rights law, focusing on human rights violations in the work place. I also have an interest in refugee law and children in warfare. I can't seem to stop thinking and obsessing about a world that looks to be heading for imminent destruction. I spend a lot of time trying to figure out where I can do 'damage control,' hoping to derive some peace from easing the suffering of a few."

If I do nothing else at Georgetown Law, I want to be certain that my teaching reinforces the ideals of a student like that. Stories help, ones of lawyers who are other-centered people, not self-centered.

I tell of visiting Belle Glade, Florida, one of the most dispirited towns in America. It is surrounded by canefields, vast flatlands owned by sugar corporations that control local politics like medieval fiefs. The workers might as well be serfs. During the six-month cutting season—from October to March—their wages are low, they have no union, they live in shacks and hovels, and they are part of a work force that has one of the nation's highest injury and turnover rates. The misery is such that Americans will not do the work.

No problem, say the owners. They bring in ten thousand blacks from Jamaica, and if they don't like life in Belle Glade they can go back home. Ten thousand more are ready to come. I spent some time interviewing the cutters. One after another told me about a lawyer in the town. He had been there for years. Other lawyers had come to Belle Glade with visions of reform, but they didn't last. Progress was slow, results minimal. They soon left, drained emotionally. But this one lawyer who stayed was different. I could tell that the Jamaicans revered him.

I went to find him at his office. He had scruffy, unkempt hair, a restless mien. He wore a faded tee shirt, muddy dungarees, and unpolished shoes. He didn't look or smell like your average K Street lawyer. During the season he often worked between seventy and eighty hours a week taking care of the workers' injuries claims, suing the companies for past abuses, and researching facts on current ones. His Florida Rural Legal Services salary was under thirty thousand dollars. I asked him why he came to Belle Glade and why he stayed. The answer was memorable: "I wake up every morning and can say to myself honestly that if I wasn't here doing this work it wouldn't get done."

No higher praise can be given about a person's labor. Most people are easily replaced. But this lawyer knew he could not be. That knowledge served as compensation, making up for whatever his paycheck lacked. I became curious about the lawyer's background. He had a Harvard law degree. I thought to myself, he's out of Harvard Law fifteen years and has only a peanuts salary? Maybe he's been disbarred. Must be. I joked with him about it.

On returning to Washington, and wanting to write about this lawyer—I had met few like him—I called up Harvard Law and found a dean who remembered him. His grades were spotty, the dean recalled. He was forever hanging around soup kitchens, migrant-worker camps, union halls, and battered women's shelters. He didn't come to class much and on those rare days he did he often left muttering about how boring law school was. The day he graduated, the peg in the faculty lounge about him was that here was someone who came to Harvard Law School and learned little about the law but learned much about justice. He's been invited back several times to speak about the rewards of public-interest law, because that's where lawyers are needed. An estimated 70 percent of America's lawyers work for 10 percent of the population, and Jamaican cane cutters aren't among them.

After learning of Kevin's West Point and Marine Corps background, and his renunciation of the military ethic, I wasn't surprised that he wanted to have a class on Tolstoy. The Russian also had been a soldier and had returned home to embrace pacifism. It happens often. The list of former warriors-turned-pacifists includes Howard Zinn, Philip Berrigan, Garry Davis, Heinrich Böll, Jacques de Bollardiere, and Francis of Assisi. Howard Zinn, a World War II bombardier, became a voice for nonviolence: "I had moved away from my own rather orthodox view that there are just wars and unjust wars, to a universal rejection of war as a solution to any human problem." Phil Berrigan, also a World War II combatant, believes

> there will be no healing for veterans, myself included, until we disavow war completely, until we disarm the bomb and the killing machine and ourselves. Why are we alive except to unmask the Big Lie of War? Where are the veterans from all the empire's wars in the struggle for disarmament, for justice, for peace? They should ask themselves, "Can I remedy my violence, can I heal myself until I try to heal the body of humankind from the curse of war?"

Only a few in the room are familiar with the writings of Zinn and Berrigan. Kevin Allen is one.

We prepare for the class on Tolstoy by reading two excerpts from *War and Peace*—one on Napoleon's indifference to the suffering of his soldiers, the other a battlefield scene in which French and Russian troops take time out to fraternize with each other as the human beings they knew themselves to be, not martialized enemies—and the essays "Patriotism or Peace?," "Letter to a Corporal," and "Advice to a Draftee," plus a three-thousand-word biographical essay on Tolstoy's life. Only two in the class had read *War and Peace*. One had read part of *Anna Karenina*. None is familiar with the essays. None is aware that Tolstoy and Gandhi corresponded with each other, an exchange of letters in the early twentieth century when Gandhi was early middle-aged and an elderly Tolstoy neared his end. The correspondence was gathered into a book by Martin Green, a professor at Tufts. Kevin Allen took notes on that.

In "Patriotism or Peace?" Tolstoy equates personal egotism with national egotism. Egomaniacs who are self-absorbed, who boast in subtle or obvious ways about their superiority, are seen as irrational, while collectively a nation can do the same and claim it as patriotism. In foreign-policy speeches, U.S. presidents routinely state that America is the world's superpower, it is Number One, it is the strongest nation on earth. "Our nation," proclaims George W. Bush, "is chosen by God and commissioned by history to be a model for the world." Madeleine Albright asserted: "If we have to use force, it is because we are America! We are the indispensable nation!"

Tolstoy's argument is that patriotism masks militarism. In class I ask Kevin Allen to read aloud a paragraph from "Patriotism or Peace?"

What produces war is the desire for an exclusive good for one's own nation—what is called patriotism. And so to abolish war, it is necessary to abolish patriotism, and to abolish patriotism, it is necessary first to become convinced that it is an evil, and that is hard to do. Tell people that war is bad, and they will laugh at you: who does not know that? Tell them that patriotism is bad, and the majority of people will agree with you, but with a small proviso. "Yes, patriotism is bad but there is another patriotism, the one we adhere to." But wherein this good patriotism consists no one can explain. . . . Patriotism cannot be good. Why do not people say that egotism can be good, though this may be asserted more easily, because egotism is a natural sentiment, with which man is born, while patriotism is an unnatural sentiment which is artificially inoculated in him?

Not everyone in the class is buying, for sure.

"It's possible to be patriotic," someone says, "and not be militaristic."

"How?"

"By promoting a country's virtues and working to eliminate its vices."

"But shouldn't that be done by everyone everywhere, regardless of where, merely by accident, he or she happened to be born?"

"So I was born in America. I do it here."

"But why think of yourself as only a citizen of America and not as a citizen of the world?"

"Because I live here."

"But *here* was Earth long before it was named America."

Right about now, I'm wishing Tolstoy were with us. The debate goes on for awhile, with four or five joining in and the rest listening and mulling. What's in the mullers' minds? I won't know until next April when I read their evaluations of the course, when perhaps they will say that I had class favorites—the ones who agreed with that old bitter pill Tolstoy—or that I was a propagandist pushing an agenda. Or. Or. Or. Or.

As the debate over patriotism tapers off, I refer the class to a handout I passed around earlier: a collection of quotes from Tolstoy that are similar to ones expressed by a sampling of other believers in nonviolence. "Read them on your own," I suggest, "and make your own judgments on whether Tolstoy's ideas are relevant to our own times."

♦ From *War and Peace,* Part X, Chapter xxv, Prince Andrei speaking:

> *But what is war? What is needed for success in war-fare? What are the habits of the military? The aim of war is murder; the methods of war are spying, treachery, and their encouragement, the ruin of a country's inhabitants, robbing them or stealing to provision the army, and fraud and falsehood termed military craft. The habits of the military class are the absence of*

freedom, that is, discipline, idleness, ignorance, cruelty, debauchery, and drunkenness. And in spite of all this, it is the highest class, respected by everyone. And he who kills the most people receives the highest.

♦ From a Studs Terkel interview of (Ret.) Admiral Gene LaRocque, founder and longtime director of the Center for Defense Information in Washington:

[In World War II] I had been in thirteen battle engagements, had sunk a submarine, and was the first man ashore in the landing at Roi. In that four years, I thought, what a hell of a waste of a man's life. I lost a lot of friends. I had the task of telling my roommate's parents about our last days together. You lose limbs, sight, part of your life—for what? Old men send young men to war. Flags, banners, and patriotic sayings. . . . We've institutionalized militarism. This came out of World War II. It gave us the National Security Council. It gave us the CIA, which is able to spy on you and me this very moment. For the first time in the history of man, a country has divided up the world into military districts. I hate it when they say, "He gave his life for his country." Nobody gives his life for anything. We steal the lives of these kids. We take it away from them. They don't die for the honor and glory of their country. We kill them.

♦ From "Letter to a Corporal":

It has been impressed upon [soldiers] that the oath which they are compelled to take upon entering military service is obligatory for them, and that they may not kill men in general, but may kill them by command of the authorities. . . . But here arises the question. How can people of sound mind, who frequently know the rudiments and are even educated, believe in such a palpable lie? No matter how little educated a man may be, he nonetheless cannot help knowing that Christ did not permit any murder, but taught meekness, humility, forgiveness of offenses, love of enemies; he cannot help but see that, on the basis of Christian teaching, he cannot make a promise in advance that he will kill all those whom he is commanded to kill.

* From "We Won't Go" by Stephen Fortunato, Jr.:
I came to conscientious objection over a somewhat circuitous route, via the Marine Corps. With all the passion and exuberance of youth I became a trained killer. I went to classes where I learned how to rip a man's jugular vein out with my teeth. I growled like a tiger when I was told to growl like a tiger.
    I was told that the Ten Commandments, however worthy they might be in civilian life, had to be suspended in the name of national interest. I was greatly impressed to see that an act perpetrated by the enemy was ipso facto vicious and deceitful, whereas the same act perpetrated by the United States was just and praiseworthy.

* From *War and Peace*:
Government is an association of men who do violence to the rest of us.

* From I. F. Stone:
All governments are run by liars.

* From Tolstoy's *The Kingdom of God Is within You*:
Christ could certainly not have established the Church. That is, the institution we now call by that name, for nothing resembling our present conception of the Church—with its sacraments, its hierarchy, and especially its claim to infallibility—is to be found in Christ's words or in the conception of the men of his time.

♦ From a sermon by Phillips Brooks:
*In the best sense of the word, Jesus was a radical. His
religion has so long been identified with conservatism
that it is almost startling sometimes to remember that
all the conservatives of his own times were against
him: that it was the young, free, restless, sanguine,
progressive part of the people who flocked to him.*

♦ From Henry David Thoreau:
*If Christ should appear on earth he would on all hands
be denounced as a mistaken, misguided man, insane
and crazed.*

"Browse around some old used bookstores," I advise the
class before leaving, "and look for Tolstoy. You'll have a lifetime of worthy reading." If anyone in the class is likely to
begin building a Tolstoy library, it is Kevin Allen.

Oak Hill

A rarity—a white boy is here. He's the first I've seen in
three years. Jared is seventeen, slender, with a mop of blond
hair that flops over his forehead. He was in his third year of
public high school in suburban Maryland. When introducing
myself to him I ask how long he thought he'd be here. Just a
few days, he says, with some confidence. He has a good
lawyer. Jared says he might be phoning any minute.

Not many of the blacks are in Oak Hill for "just a few days,"
and I'm not sure how many have attentive lawyers. Most are
court appointed, with heavy caseloads. Nearly every week
at least one boy asks me to a put in a good word with the
judge that sent him here and who has power to release him
early. Few of the boys have faith in their lawyers.

Last April the Justice Department reported that among
juvenile offenders jailed for the first time, blacks are six times
more likely to be incarcerated than whites. On drug convictions blacks are forty-eight times more likely than whites to

end up in a juvenile prison. For violent crimes: an average 254 days for blacks, and 193 days for whites.

Is racism at work? Many on the Left believe that young blacks are easy prey for tough prosecutors who want to clear the street of thugs. Or are dysfunctional families and violent neighborhoods the cause? The Right holds that stable blacks are glad to see young drug dealers and gunmen locked up for long stretches.

If I were still writing newspaper columns, I'd jump in to argue round or argue square and quickly move on to the next issue and the heady joys of more abstract pondering. But now I have four living, wary, and desperately needy kids in front of me, not one of them an abstraction much less an issue. Suddenly, Justice Department reports on sentencing inequalities seem remote.

We do the Kind Word Exercise. This week Kathleen Maloy and Jeff Schroeder, two of my Washington Center students from Bowling Green State University in Ohio, have come. They are sweethearts, with plans to marry and join the Peace Corps after graduating in May. When Ronald, sitting next to Kathleen, has his turn for a kind word, he grins widely and says, "I think you're pretty." Cheering erupts.

For an exercise I pass around a paper with five questions;

1. What three things are you really good at?
2. What would you like to become better at?
3. How do you work out disagreements with somebody?
4. Name two people you have recently forgiven.
5. Do you find it easy or hard to forgive someone who has hurt you?

The answers to number one are strikingly similar for the Oak Hill boys:
Ronald: Football, carpentry, boxing
Andre: Basketball, rapping, writing
Dwayne: Basketball, football, sex
Rodney: Basketball, football, baseball

Jared, the boy from Montgomery County, obviously has a different background.

Jared: Teaching concepts, peaceful conflict resolution, procrastinating

Kathleen: Critical thinking, ice skating, writing

Jeff: Remaining calm, obviating

Number two: What would you like to become better at?

Ronald: Basketball, reading, staying away from Oak Hill

Andre: Solving school problems, work

Dwayne: Working on computers

Rodney: Carpentry

Jared: Long-distance running

Kathleen: Not letting others upset me, keeping in contact with my friends and family, doing more community service

Jeff: Being patient, communicating with people

Number three: How do you work out disagreements?

Ronald: I talk to them or stay away from them

Andre: Talk about it

Dwayne: Try to talk to them or walk away

Rodney: Talk

Jared: Peacefully

Kathleen: I try to understand why the other person is upset, talk things out, and try not to raise my voice

Jeff: Empathize with them and try to get them to understand my position

Number four: Two people you have recently forgiven.

Ronald: My baby, my mother, myself

Andre: Nobody

Dwayne: My mother, my caseworker

Rodney: My mother and sister

Jared: My girlfriend, Jenny

Kathleen: Jim, myself

Jeff: Myself, my friend Brian

Number five: Do you find it easy or hard to forgive someone who has hurt you?

Ronald: Hard

Andre: Sometime it is hard to forgive people that hurt you, but you will have to move on

Dwayne: Easy at times but almost always hard

Rodney: No, not hard

Jared: This depends on certain variables

Kathleen: Pretty hard depending on the situation

Jeff: Very difficult

No one had trouble expanding on his or her answers. Andre, who said that he has forgiven nobody, was shot not long before he came to Oak Hill. He spoke of it—a leg wound—casually. Across the circle Ronald said two years ago he took a bullet in the back. He pulled up his shirt. The dime-sized hole had healed and could have passed for a large freckle. Both boys knew the person who shot them, which, they said, made forgiveness harder—because he couldn't be forgotten.

The thinking behind the exercise is to get the boys to begin noticing what they think and do. The idea is self-reflection. Without that ability, their time at Oak Hill may be no more than months and years of watching their back, angling for petty advantages, looking for more reasons to be angry. Self-reflection, which is essential both for personality development and change, is hard at any age, but it is especially hard in adolescence and, more especially, during incarcerated adolescence. Among prisoners, self-reflection, if it ever happens at all, comes after years and years of hard time. Look at the lives of black authors such as Carl Upchurch, Nathan McCall, Claude Brown, and Malcolm X. Each had a horrible childhood, each was arrested, convicted, and locked away early in life. Only after years and years did they finally see the sense in being able to notice their own thoughts and acts; that was the breakthrough to taking responsibility for their decisions, to figuring out the consequences before acting.

Maybe I'm asking too much of the boy prisoners at Oak Hill. These kids need job training, basic reading skills, drug therapy, and career counseling, plus intensive follow-up supervision when they leave here. All too probably they will have no easy time surviving in a society that sees them as predatory thugs.

And I'm trying to get them to be self-reflective, as if they're novices in a Buddhist ashram?

It's either that or give up on them totally. And say that we'll never, never have another Carl Upchurch, Nathan McCall, Claude Brown, or Malcolm X. And say that once a person is sent to prison, no chance exists for a comeback.

I'm not ready to believe that.

School Without Walls

A Danish exchange student has joined the class, a girl, fifteen, named Katja. I ask her if she can name ten cities in the United States. She can and does. I ask the American students to name two cities in Denmark. None can. Tentatively, two come up with Copenhagen. I ask Katja which countries border the United States. "Canada and Mexico," she says. I ask the Americans which country or countries border Denmark. No one knows.

Whenever an international student—I avoid the term foreign student—is in a class, I do this little geography exercise. Rarely is an American knowledgeable about the country the new classmate is from. Almost always the international student knows the cities, borders, and rivers of the United States. The American kids get the point: become globalists, move beyond the provincialism of Americocentrism, learn about the world. Are we Earthlans or Americans?

The kids are feeling playful. They ask, "Time for another one-hundred-dollar-bill quiz?"

"Let's," I answer, pulling out my ever-crisp Ben Franklin and standing it on the desk. "Make it an easy quiz," the kids parry, gaping at the bill.

"I'll make it so easy you'll feel insulted."

The quiz: Identify the following five living beings. All either live or work within three miles of Walls.

"What's the name of Bill and Hillary Clinton's cat?"

All hands rise. "Socks," they call out.

"You're one for one. Next, what's the name of their dog?"

All hands rise. "Buddy."

"You're two for two. Next, name the chairman of the Senate Armed Services Committee, where military contractors go to keep the money flowing for new weapons programs and are warmly welcomed."

No one knows.

"Next, name the chairman of Senate Judiciary Committee, where legal loopholes get written that favor the powerful."

No one knows. Someone guesses: "Henry Hyde, that guy with the white hair who was out to get Clinton?"

"Good try, nix."

"Next, name the chairman of the Senate Energy Committee, where oil, timber, and coal companies show up to sugar their deals."

No one knows.

As I put away my always safe one-hundred-dollar bill, they're groaning: "You call that an easy quiz?"

Another asks, "What's the point of the quiz?"

Not hammering too hard, I tell them it's time to wake up and learn where the power is, who's using it, who benefits and who doesn't, and forget about Socks and Buddy. I tell the boys that when they turn eighteen, the game begins. "You'll be told to register for the draft. And told, also, to obey, because that's the law and because it's noble to serve your country by being in the military."

Pacifists and believers in nonviolence have a different slant on that. Those in the military aren't serving their country, they're serving those who are *running* the country—a large difference, because those who are running the country, including many of the chairmen of Senate committees, give little sign of concern about schools. If they did, Walls would have a cafeteria, a gym, and better paid teachers. They show little concern about poor people. If they did, heat grates three blocks away, in front of the State Department, wouldn't be covered every winter night with the homeless and the mad. They show little concern about public safety. If they did, the risk of suffering a major gunshot wound in Washington's poorest neighborhoods would not dramatically increase after age of twelve.

"OK," the class said, "tell us who all those Senate chairman are."

"Sorry," I answer. "If I tell you, you'll forget. If you look it up, you'll remember. And if you remember, maybe you'll begin reading the sports section and the comics less, and begin reading the national and international news sections more. Then you'll recognize the names of people in power and begin asking how that power is being used."

My crack about newspaper reading habits isn't a hit, especially since I've been repeating it all semester. Every morning a pile of free copies of *The Washington Post* sits on a table near the school entrance, there for the taking. Sometimes half the papers remain. At lunch break—in the classrooms—I notice that the students who did pick up a copy are mostly scanning the sports and comics pages. I asked my own class at the beginning of the year which part of the paper they think is the most relevant to their lives. Their brows having been well beaten by my bents for national and international news, they said national and international news.

Almost. The most relevant section is the letters-to-the-editor page: "That's your page. Take time to write a letter to the *Post* on an issue you know and care about. Even if it isn't published, you've made the effort. Then try again with another letter."

The smallness of the class—fewer than ten students gives the feel of a private school—creates an easygoing atmosphere, with room for both focused discussions and the occasional playful digression, which sometimes has a point. In

my classes I announce in the opening week that I allow myself one privilege: a digression every class. Just one. I appoint an official digression watcher to stop me if I start a
second.

Today's digression: Newspapers ought to pay readers
whose letters are published. The larger the circulation, the
higher the fee. Some of the most clearheaded writing in newspapers is found on the letters page, yet the papers get away
with paying nothing.

The capitalist wing of the class endorses that idea.

After the digression—my dream is to become such a skilled
digressor that the official digression watcher won't realize
until long after the class that I actually slipped in a second
one—time to get past the warmups. The presence of Katja,
the Danish girl, in class is an opportunity, as golden as it
gets. Eight or ten weeks into the course—at this school and
the others—someone can be counted on to say that "nonviolence is fine in theory but where has it actually worked?"
Often the question is twinned with another supposed stop-
per: "Do you really think nonviolence would have worked
against Hitler?"

I've never given a classroom answer that came close to
satisfying either the questioner or me. Sound bites don't do
it. I feel like a math teacher who chalks the blackboard with
calculus equations and then a student—who has never taken
a math course before and has been told all his life that
$2+2=423$—rises to say that nothing on the board makes
sense. But make it clear with a quickie answer. Right now.

A full semester, or two or three, could be given over to
examples where nonviolence worked. But for the next two
hours we examine just one: the Danish resistance to Hitler's
army in the early 1940s.

I pass around Thomas Merton's essay "Danish Nonviolent
Resistance to Hitler." In nine hundred words it offers a suc-
cinct analysis of how nearly an entire population success-
fully carried out a method of defiance that had nothing to do
with killing German people. Denmark, Merton writes,

*was one of the only nations which offered explicit,
formal and successful nonviolent resistance to Nazi
power. The adjectives are important. The resistance
was successful because it was explicit and formal, and
because it was practically speaking unanimous. The
entire Danish nation simply refused to cooperate with
the Nazis, and resisted every move of the Nazis against
the Jews with nonviolent protest of the highest and
most effective caliber, yet without any need for organization, training, or specialized activism: simply by
unanimously and effectively expressing in word and
action the force of their deeply held moral convictions.*

Led by King Christian X, who took daily horseback rides
through the streets of Copenhagen during the Nazi occupa-
tion, escorted by bicycling citizens, the Danes organized an
effective unarmed bloc of resistance. By strikes, work slow-
downs, refusals to repair German ships in their shipyards,
and hiding or helping Jews to flee, they calmly and efficiently
defied the Nazi invaders.

I ask Michael Henry to read aloud the first lines from Gene
Sharp's essay "The Technique of Nonviolent Action," ones
that express the philosophy of resistance:

*A ruler's power is ultimately dependent on support
from the people he would rule. His moral authority,
economic resources, transport system, government
bureaucracy, army and police—to name but a few
sources of his power—rest finally upon the cooperation
and assistance of other people. If there is general
conformity, the ruler is powerful. But people do not
always do what their rulers would have them do.*

The class discussion is on rules that the students either reject or accept every day, a theory as basic to their own lives as
it once was to the Danes. Whenever they walk onto school
property, their implied unspoken message to administrators—

the immediate government—is this: Order me around, I will obey. Tell me which classroom to report to, I will go. Tell me when to turn in a paper, I will turn it in. Tell me when school starts, I will be there. Tell me when school is over, I'll leave. You order, I obey. You command, I cooperate.*

In addition to the Merton essay I bring to class a VCR tape of a PBS documentary that was televised in September 2000: "A Force More Powerful: A Century of Nonviolent Conflict." With a blend of archival footage, eyewitness testimony, and a crisp journalistic narrative that remains nonideological throughout, the story is told that violent force is not the only force. A more powerful and more effective one exists. Out of dozens of twentieth-century examples the filmmakers chose six nonviolent campaigns in which organized citizen resistance, noncooperation, and direct action defeated governmental oppression: student sit-ins in Nashville during the U.S. civil rights movement; Gandhi's thirty-two-year effort to remove the British from India; Solidarity's strikes in Poland that

---

* The most recent display of students' withdrawing cooperation occurred in the spring semester at Berkeley High School in California, when members of the class of 2000 and 2001 staged a mass walkout. Their grievances—well stated before the protest—included an incompetent college admissions counselor, underpaid and over-worked teachers, and Proposition 21, the Juvenile Justice Initiative. The latter, on the March 7 ballot, proposed lowering the age for juveniles to be tried in the adult courts from sixteen to fourteen, expanding mandatory sentencing, limiting alternative methods of juvenile rehabilitation, and increasing crimes eligible for the death penalty. The California salary for correctional officers is $51,000, for first-year teachers $28,000. An editorial in the student newspaper entitled "Berkeley High in Turmoil" supported the walkout. Students have a basic right "that their transcripts actually get sent to colleges. Teachers aren't focusing on their lesson plans. They're debating tactics, planning boycotts and discussing the possibility of a strike. . . . Our school is falling apart." The protest had mixed results. The main college admissions counselor was fired, and the faculty began pulling itself together. Proposition 21, meant to control what one conservative politician called "young super predators"—passed 62 percent to 38 percent).

ousted the Soviet puppet regime; the consumer boycotts that led to the end of apartheid in South Africa; public demands in the 1980s to free elections in Chile that removed the Pinochet regime; and the Danish resistance.

The section on the Danish resistance is twenty-five minutes. In it, a postwar historian summarizes the defiance: "Denmark had not won the war but neither had it been defeated or destroyed. Most Danes had not been brutalized, by the Germans or by each other. Nonviolent resistance saved the country and contributed more to the Allied victory than Danish arms could ever have done."

The educational value of "A Force More Powerful" is in its factual challenge to prevailing misconceptions, beginning with the notion that nonviolent resistance equals passive resistance. "It's not a semantic distinction," says Peter Ackerman, one of the film's consultants. "It is the critical difference between action and inaction. What Gandhi did and what the people in Chile did and what Lech Walesa did was anything but passive. They just didn't sit there. They went out and did proactive things. . . . People in nonviolent struggles are not unarmed. They are simply not armed with violent weapons. But make no mistake, they have formidable resources that flow from the fabric of their society."

Our *Solutions to Violence* text has a full chapter devoted to resistance to the Nazis. It centers on Le Chambon, the French village that was one of Europe's leading centers for hiding and rescuing Jews and which was led by pacifist Huguenot pastors. One of the essays is "The Town That Defied the Holocaust" by Grace Yoder, another "Lest Innocent Blood Be Shed" by Philip Hallie. The story of Le Chambon is about a conscience-driven community that collectively decided that, unlike other towns in the area of south central France, it would not take up guns if and when the Germans came. Le Chambon survived with few casualties. Those towns that relied on violent resistance suffered massive deaths.

Long after the war Philip Hallie, a professor at Wesleyan University, interviewed Andre Trocme, one of the pacifist pastors. He had searched out a former Nazi military officer who was in the area of Le Chambon. Trocme inquired why the Germans spared his village. Le Chambon had a type of resistance, he said, that had "nothing to do with anything we could destroy with violence." The villagers had weapons of the spirit, which proved superior to the Nazis' weapons of steel.

In the late 1980s Pierre Sauvage, a Los Angeles filmmaker who was born in Le Chambon to Jewish refugees in 1943, produced a documentary, *Weapons of the Spirit,* that has become a classic antiwar film. I use if often in my classes. Students never failed to be moved by it.

Skepticism often remains, which I welcome. Students with Jewish backgrounds who have had grandparents or other relatives killed in the death camps tend to be eloquent in expressing their misgivings about pacifism and nonviolent resistance. For them, I can do no better than to say that other Jews, with equal eloquence, have embraced nonviolence. There is Erwin Knoll, the editor of *The Progressive,* who died in 1994 and for whose magazine I write and to which I encourage my students to subscribe if they want to be revved to take action to create a just society. Erwin Knoll's contribution to the literature of peace is on view in "Not a Just War, Just a War," a short essay he wrote for *The Progressive* in June 1991 and which I have given all my students ever since:

> *I was born in Austria, and at the age of six I watched jackbooted Nazi troops march into Vienna. Millions of Austrians cheered. I was fortunate to escape with my life, but many members of my family weren't that lucky. They died in the camps. The Holocaust is, I suppose, the formative experience of my life.*
>
> *As a teenager, even as a young adult, I loved to go to old World War II films so I could watch the Germans die. It gave me special pleasure to see the violent end inevitably allotted to officers of the Waffen SS who invariably wore monocles, permanent sneers, and black uniforms adorned with swastikas and death's-*

head insignia. I assumed, somehow, that all the German soldiers who froze to death in the siege of Stalingrad and all the German civilians cremated in the firestorm bombing of Dresden were officers of the Waffen SS who wore monocles, black uniforms, and permanent sneers. It took me an embarrassingly long time to figure out that wasn't the case. Apparently, some people still haven't figured it out.

But wasn't it necessary, after all, to stop Hitler? Sure it was. It was necessary, in fact, not to let him get started. But of all the ways to stop Hitler or to keep him from getting started, war was the worst—the way that inflicted the most pain, the most suffering, the most damage on everyone—especially Hitler's victims. A few months ago, when I read and reviewed Howard Zinn's latest book, Declarations of Independence, I was deeply moved by the account of his moral and intellectual journey from World War II bombardier to pacifist. Zinn offers persuasive evidence that the war magnified rather than diminished Nazi atrocities. And he writes, "History is full of instances of successful resistance— although we are not informed very much about this— without violence and against tyranny, by people using strikes, boycotts, propaganda, and a dozen ingenious forms of struggle."

I believe in ingenious, nonviolent struggle for justice and against oppression. So I won't support our troops— not in the Persian Gulf or anywhere else. And I won't support anyone else's troops when they go about their murderous business. And I'll say, regrettably, to the fallen black soldiers of the 54th Massachusetts, and the guys dead on the beaches of Normandy, and the young people who threw stones at Brezhnev's tanks in the streets of Czechoslovakia, that they died in vain perpetuating a cycle of human violence that must be stopped, because there is no such thing as a just war. Never was. Never will be.

At noon Katja leaves the class smiling. Understandably. We've learned about her homeland and some of its heroic believers in nonviolence, as she has learned about some of America's: Thomas Merton, Gene Sharp, Peter Ackerman, Erwin Knoll, Howard Zinn. Different lands, same ideals.

December

Power With, Not Power Over

Establishing lasting peace is the work of education. All politics can do is keep us out of war.

—Maria Montessori

Traditional education glorifies established political power that uses brute force to oppress people and legitimize its authority. History books praise military heroes and ignore the contributions of peacemakers. Violence is carried on by governments oppressing weaker nations and exhibited in homes where physical assault is used in situations of conflict, disobedience, anger, and frustration. Structural violence condemns people to substandard levels of existence, while educational systems support those structures that contribute to the militarization of social life. Peace education questions the structures of violence that dominate everyday life and tries to create a peaceful disposition to counteract the omnipotent values of militarism.

—Ian Harris

Stone Ridge

Seventy miles north of the placid, secure, and carefully gardened campus of Stone Ridge is the Hagerstown, Maryland, state prison that holds Philip Berrigan behind its walls. He is midway through a thirty-month stretch for conspiring to damage two A-10 Warthog warplanes at the Air National Guard base in Middle River, Maryland, and then doing the damage in the predawn hours of December 19, 1999. The damage— a few hammer bangs—was more symbolic than real. It is one of a long list of convictions going back to the late 1960s, when he and his Jesuit brother Daniel, found their life's work in resisting the military world order. Both are in their mid-seventies now, defiers of mellowness and nurturers of friends and allies on the fringes.

In the literature of nonviolence both Berrigans have been like reporters covering the peace zones, whether in court-rooms explaining their unabated breaking of laws that sanction war-making or from the prisons where they are punished for what Daniel calls "the fracture of good order."

In his *Book of Uncommon Prayer*, Daniel writes:

> *We are malign enough, twisted enough, to bring creation to a smoking ruin.*
> *—we have the instruments.*
> *—we have the myths.*
> *—we even have the blueprints.*
> *They are stashed away in some war room, in some hollowed out mountain. Who will confront this crime? I think it is only the resisting people. Those who confront weapons, weapons-maker and their immaculate guardian—the law. If a God exists, these are God's people.*

Only occasionally is a student familiar with one of the Berrigans, and rarely both. This month, with this class, some remedial work is in order. I ask that Philip Berrigan's 1970 essay be read, "Can We Serve Both Love and War?" After thirty years its twelve hundred words are aging well, as crisp and relevant as when written during the bloodletting of Vietnam. Philip was then in the Danbury, Connecticut, federal prison for destroying draft records in Catonsville, Maryland, in 1968. It is impossible, he writes, to serve both love and war:

People have two problems when they try to serve love. The first is to know themselves; the second is to know what they must be. As to the first, we are, in effect, a violent people and none of the mythological pabulum fed us at Mother's knee, in the classroom, or at Fourth of July celebrations can refute the charge. The evidence is too crushing, whether it be Hiroshima, or nuclear equivalents of seven tons of TNT for every person on this planet, or scorched earth in the Iron Triangle, or Green Berets in Guatemala, or subhuman housing in the ghettoes of America. A substantial share of our trouble comes from what we own, and how we regard what we own. President Johnson told our troops: "They [the rest of the world] want what we have and we're not going to give it to them."

I'm not sure if the references to the Vietnam war connect with the students. I ask how many had a parent who fought in Southeast Asia in the 1960s and 1970s. None did. I'm reminded of a *New Yorker* cartoon, with a father sitting in the living room saying to his little boy, "Son, everyone went to college in the sixties—there was a war going on." Berrigan's essay runs deep with strong sentiments, ones that might put many in the class on the defensive should they choose to reflect on the comparative wealth in which they have grown up. Berrigan, I offer, is not trying to make us feel guilty but to feel responsible:

When a people arbitrarily decides that this planet and its riches are to be divided unequally, among equals, and that the only criterion for the division is the amount of naked power at its disposal, diplomacy tends to be essentially military, truth tends to be fiction, and war

> *tends to be the ultimate rationality, because reason has been bankrupted of human alternatives.*
>
> *This tells us something about what we are economically and politically, if not personally. And yet the personal integrity of each one of us is indissolubly linked with our social integrity. In truth, the two cannot be separated. This means that it is useless to oppose the violence in Vietnam while refusing to face personal violence in its every manifestation: bias, arrogance, insensitivity, dislikes, indiscriminate sensuality, trivial values.*

Berrigan makes the pro-consistency, anti-selectivity argument. If any group is likely to pick up on it, it is high school seniors. They have had their fill of adult double standards and are beginning to work on their own. In her paper on "Can We Serve Both Love and War?" a girl on her way to Duke applies Berrigan's ideas to the politics of the day. That politicians can support violence in one place while trying to stop it in another is an "attitude illustrated by presidential candidate Al Gore in a town hall forum two months ago. Gore stated that he would increase the amount of money being devoted to military spending. He later responded to a series of questions about domestic violence and media promoters of violence by saying that he would support measures taken to reduce the number of deaths resulting from violence within the United States. He failed to realize that he, too, was promoting violence, by advocating it as a means of negotiation with foreign countries."

Most of the papers are admiring of Berrigan's essay, but not all. One girl—self-confident, a relisher of class debates, and refreshingly skeptical of all party lines, including the pacifists' and mine—brings up Berrigan's conviction in Catonsville. I am surprised she knew of it. One of her teachers at Holy Child, it turns out, had assigned a Daniel Berrigan essay on the Catonsville trial. "The acts of violence by the Berrigan brothers and the Catonsville Nine through burning draft records and destroying equipment," she wrote, "is by no means a representation of serving love. . . . It is hard not to respect a man like Philip Berrigan because he has such a strong argument and he even has the facts to back it up, yet his actions in Catonsville prove him to be extreme and his tactics to be rash."

The student isn't the only one with misgivings. The Left and the Far Left have been torn for decades. Some see the deeds of the Berrigans and those joining them in what are called Ploughshares Actions—civil disobedience or, more accurately, civil resistance—as street theater that leads to nothing except satisfying the miscreants' need for attention. What have the Berrigans' years of imprisonment accomplished? Others—I am with this group—see them in a long line of prophets, going back to Amos, Isaiah, Buddha, and others who believed in the value of witness, and in paying heed only to the idea that being faithful matters more than being successful.

A story is told about the Buddhist spiritual master who went to the village square everyday. He sat down and from sunrise to sunset cried out against war and injustice. This went on for years. His disciples began worrying about their spiritual master, worrying being an important duty of discipleship. Deciding to take action, they went to their master and told him he was having no effect. None at all. No one in the village was listening. "Everyone's insane," they told him. "It's time to stop." "No," said the spiritual master, "I will keep crying out against war and injustice so I won't go insane."

With students' permission, I send their papers to Phil Berrigan in the Hagerstown, Maryland, state prison. A week later a reply comes back—gracious and thankful. "When I read that 1970 essay of mine—I had forgotten writing it—I thought laughingly, 'Gawd!, he hasn't learned a thing since.' But the kids' responses were well grounded and sophisticated. Thanks for sending them. I read everything they wrote."

In my letter to Phil, I asked about the possibilities of bringing my Stone Ridge students to the prison for a visit. He gave me the names of two officials to contact. I wondered also if we could be given a talk by Father Stephen Kelly, a New York Jesuit who was given twenty-seven months for taking part in the Warthog action. "Unfortunately," Phil wrote, "[Kelly] is in the 'hole' for six months, for again refusing a random urine test. He also lost 120 days good time and a year's visits. The turnkeys here play hardball."

We never visited Phil. Shortly after, he was transferred to a prison in Ohio.

School Without Walls

Students are customers, teachers are sellers. But what if the seller doesn't give the customers their full money's worth?

Last week, I didn't. I came to class unprepared, distracted and ready to wing it. The kids will never know the difference, I thought. Show them a film, the great time-eater.

By way of small amends, I begin this week's class asking if anyone noticed that last week my game was off, way off. We did jump around a bit more than usual, one says. Another agrees. "You're right," I level with them. "I let you down."

Whether or not my admission means anything, I take out of my wallet nine five-dollar bills and give one to each student. By rough estimate, five dollars is about what the students' parents pay in taxes for my class every week. The kids look at the five-dollar bills, as if maybe they're fake.

If customers aren't receiving all they paid for, return their money. Why shouldn't the education industry be held to the same standard found in others?

It's bleaker in college. At American University, where I will have a course next semester, the total bill currently tops thirty-two thousand dollars. And that's a middle tier school, with costs well under the upper tier. The stony reality that college is expensive remains an abstraction to most students. Checks are sent in by parents, and loans are taken out. The remedy? Students should bring their money to school in single dollar bills stuffed into suitcases, with everyone gathering on the quad the first week of the fall semester to have Money Day. Stack the suitcases high, with payers—students and their parents—on one side, and the faculty and administrators on the other. While gazing on the suitcased loot, the visual impact would hit the customers: what are we getting for all of that?

Even better than an annual Money Day would be the Money Pile. Every class, students would come in with cash, the exact amount for that particular class on that particular day. Lay it all out in front of the professor. If the goods aren't delivered—a lively lecture, ample discussion—students can take their money back.

Back from this fantasy—it will never happen, so entrenched are the sellers and so passing-through are the buyers—I notice my Walls kids are astir. The five-dollar windfall has them thinking: why aren't all their teachers doing this? Let's have a real vouchers program.

Georgetown Law

I don't know the class sentiments on capital punishment. I prefer not to ask. Opinions about it tend to be feeling-based, not information-based. Few law schools teach death-penalty law, and at those a scant few students sign up. Even then, one or two courses aren't enough. No practice of law has fewer inducements. The pay is low, the hours long—years and years on one case—and, odds on, you'll end up watching your client die. To their credit, some of the large law firms will turn a partner loose to take on a condemned client pro bono. A fair number of the men released from death row— this week two are freed in Louisiana, making the number ninety-two in the last twenty years—had big-firm lawyers. In 1994 when the Gingrich Congress was having its moment— Newt pledged to "renew American civilization"—a $19 million federally funded program for death-penalty lawyers was destroyed. That became another reason for law students to think of other specialties.

In the hope that one or two might still want to consider death-penalty law, I give two weeks for a discussion of a death-penalty case that details the story of capital punishment in as gripping a way as any I know.

It is about Joseph Giarratano. Now forty-four, he was convicted of stabbing to death a woman and her teenaged daughter, Toni and Michelle Kline, on February 4, 1979, in a rooming-house apartment that the three shared in Norfolk, Virginia. Late in the evening of February 3, Giarratano, an alcohol and drug abuser, had come to the apartment in a half-stoned state. He blacked out on the living room sofa. In the morning he awoke to find the bodies of his two housemates, one bloodied from a slit throat, the other strangled. Assuming that he must have killed the two, but with no conscious recollection, Giarratano fled by bus to Florida. Arriving in Jacksonville and overcome with remorse and presumed guilt, he turned himself in to a cop who was eating breakfast at the bus station. He said he had just killed two people and wanted to be punished. That shouldn't be a problem, the cop said.

In a Virginia court where he was represented by an inexperienced, court-appointed lawyer, the case against Giarratano during a four-hour trial had all the markings of low-grade justice. Bloody shoe prints found in the apartment did not match Giarratano's boots, which had no blood on the soles. The stabbing and strangling were done by a right-handed person, while Giarratano is left-handed. Hair found on one of the victims did not match Giarratano's. The autopsy report was changed after Giarratano's confession to corroborate the confession. Giarratano gave five coerced dissimilar confessions. A state psychiatrist has testified that the confessions were made up—"confabulated"—as the result of Giarratano's psychotic mental state.

None of that mattered. He was declared guilty and dispatched to death row in the Mecklenburg, Virginia, state prison. That might have been the end of the story, except for Marie Deans. After her mother-in-law was slain in 1972 by an escaped prisoner, she founded Murder Victims Families for Reconciliation, a national group that has since grown to several thousand members. For more than two decades Deans has worked with hundreds of prisoners: recruiting pro bono lawyers for the under-represented, raking through trial records for procedural errors of suppressed evidence, accompanying men to their executions, and—easily the most grueling labor of all—trying to wake the half-comatose media to the abuses within the criminal injustice system. Unlike Sister Helen Prejean, who offers spiritual solace to the condemned, Deans goes further by doing the tedious and unglamorous legal research for prisoners who may have been wrongly convicted.

She did that for Giarratano. First, she had to persuade him that he might not have killed the Klines. Then she spent several years marshaling facts that convinced her that the state had condemned the wrong man. In 1998 I contacted her about Giarratano. "Go interview him," she said. A week later I was on the way to Mecklenburg, an eight-hour round trip from Washington. It was the first of eight visits I would make in the following years.

Except for the initial interview every trip I took along between sixty and one hundred of my students. The warden, a welcoming man whose humanity hadn't been dulled by the many years of doing society's dirty work of caging people, allowed Giarratano to give seminars on the intricacies of death-penalty law. It wasn't idle gab. After Marie Deans redirected his life, Giarratano, an eighth-grade dropout, began a program in self-education. He learned the art of a literate sentence, one that allowed him to be published in the *Yale Law Review* and on the *Los Angeles Times* op-ed page. In 1995 he became the first person on death row ever to write a brief—on behalf of Earl Washington, Jr., an illiterate and retarded fellow inmate who had no post-conviction lawyer—that was argued before the Supreme Court. In lower courts Giarratano's briefs were credited with winning several victories on behalf of prisoners.

I ask my Georgetown Law students if they had ever come across the case of *Edward Murray, director, Virginia Department of Corrections v. Joseph Giarratano*. None had, even though it stands as a major decision in death-penalty law. On death row Giarratano came to know Earl Washington, Jr., an illiterate, penniless inmate with an IQ of 69. If the courts of Virginia had had their death wish, Washington would have been electrocuted on September 5, 1985. In August, Washington was transferred from Mecklenburg to a small holding cell in the basement of the state penitentiary in Richmond, a facility built by the pro–death penalty Thomas Jefferson and the place where Virginia had done much of its killing.

Two weeks before Washington was to be electrocuted, Giarratano filed a civil suit in federal District Court in Virginia. He accused the state of denying the constitutional rights of indigent death-row inmates—starting with Earl Washington, Jr.—by not providing them lawyers. In addition to filing the suit, Giarratano wrote to U.S. District Court Judge Robert R. Merhige, saying that the Virginia Coalition on Jails and Prisons had appealed to more than fifty lawyers and firms to help Washington, but all had said no. Moved by the letter, Merhige himself looked for a lawyer. He found none. Giarratano, living among men who ended up on death row often because their pre-conviction lawyers were inept, unmotivated, or poorly paid, knew that post-conviction lawyers tend to be skilled and dedicated, if you had the increasingly rare luck to find one.

After a two-day trial—argued by Gerald Zerkin, a Richmond civil-liberties lawyer who had become Giarratano's appeals counsel—Earl Washington won. The state appealed and won 2-1 in the U.S. Fourth Circuit Court of Appeals. Giarratano appealed to the full court and won 6-4, a surprising victory because the Fourth is regarded as Old Dixie conservative, not known for supporting impoverished and illiterate black prisoners. The state then appealed to the Supreme Court, which took the case and heard arguments on March 22, 1989.

Giarratano wrote what it is like to be Earl Washington:

Picture yourself in this situation. You've been convicted of capital murder and sentenced to death. You are

indigent, functionally illiterate and mildly retarded.
Your court-appointed lawyer tells you that you have
the right to appeal your conviction and sentence but
that he will no longer represent you. You have been
moved into the death house. Your only choice is for
you to represent yourself. You must file something with
the court or be executed in less than 14 days. You have
the right to file a petition for certiorari or a petition for
habeas corpus and a motion for a stay of execution. But
before you can file you must learn to read, write,
overcome your retardation, obtain your trial transcript,
understand the science of law, learn how to conduct
legal research, analyze vast amounts of case law,
formulate your issues, learn all the rules, understand
civil procedure, constitutional law, criminal law and
acquire the art of legal writing. You must do all of this
and much more in less than 14 days in order to exer-
cise your right to appeal.

With Texas currently at the top of the board regarding executions, Virginia's record is overlooked. Going back to co-
lonial times, it ranks first for the total number of killed inmates. It is also the harshest regarding appeals. What Gerald
Zerkin stated in 1991 remains true a decade later: "In recent
years our state courts have reviewed about fifty cases in post-
conviction appeals and have not overturned one death sentence. Nationally, the overturn rate is more than 40 percent.
Instead of its being seen as someone's life is at stake and
therefore we need more due process, in Virginia, it's the op-
posite: because we need to kill them, we should give them
less due process."

On June 23 the Supreme Court in a 4-4 decision (with
Justice Lewis Powell not involved) ruled against Earl Washington. The due process clause of the Fourteenth Amendment and the equal protection guarantee of meaningful access to a court in the Eighth Amendment "required the state
to appoint counsel for indigent prisoners seeking post-conviction relief." Both amendments assure poor people the right

of a lawyer at the trial stage and for "an initial appeal" following sentencing. But after that, no.

Not to worry, though, said the Court, led by Chief Justice William Rehnquist, and with Justices O'Connor, Scalia, and White concurring. Virginia's prisoners should become jailhouse lawyers; that is, death-row inmates "at Mecklenburg are allowed two library periods per week." Presumably, Earl Washington and other illiterates should file suit to see if they have a Constitutional right to literacy tutors, now that they don't have a right to lawyers. They should be comforted, too, to know that had they been sentenced to die in eighteen states other than Virginia, lawyers would be provided for the entire appeal process.

In February 1991 I made what I thought could well be my last visit to Joe Giarratano. An execution date had been set for him, and he was taken from Mecklenburg to the death house in the Richmond prison. Eerily, he was the only prisoner in the building. All others had been transferred out. The ancient structure—standing for nearly two centuries in what is now prime downtown real estate—was to be demolished. Giarratano was the last prisoner there and the last to be executed in the Richmond chair. Because the main visitors' room was boarded up, I was led to the cooling room, there to have an hour's conversation with Giarratano. Cooling rooms are where prisoners' bodies go after electrocution, to chill the flesh naturally on a gurney before the mortician arrives.

We talked about the chances of the Virginia governor, L. Douglas Wilder, commuting the sentence. It wouldn't be difficult. In addition to the expected calls from the Left, including Amnesty International, which had put up billboards around the state saying an innocent man may be killed, more than twenty daily newspapers in Virginia editorialized that Giarratano's guilt was dubious and asked why he wasn't getting a new trial. James J. Kilpatrick, a conservative and long-time cheerleader for capital punishment, wrote columns asking the same question.

Confronted with all this, Wilder, a Democrat and a black who opposed the death penalty while in the state legislature but then championed it when running for governor, commuted the death sentence to life.

Why not a full pardon and freedom, or at least a new trial? Statutorily, that was a decision for the Virginia attorney general, Mary Sue Terry, a death-penalty Democrat who was then running for governor. She said that Giarratano was guilty, and that was that. Even if Terry—who would go on to lose in the fall election—had been sympathetic, there was still Rule 1.1 of the Supreme Court of Virginia—the twenty-one-day rule. Airtight, it decrees that if a capitally convicted prisoner has post-conviction evidence of innocence, the prisoner must bring it to court within twenty-one days of sentencing. After that, don't bother. Proof could exist that the accused was in Antarctica playing with penguins on the day of the crime in Virginia. After twenty-one days, it wouldn't matter. Nor would old evidence discredited by new DNA testing or other improved forensic methods. For Giarratano, as well as Earl Washington, Jr., and two others released from death row but not from prison—Herbert Bassette and Joseph Payne—Rule 1.1 effectively means a death sentence outside death row.

In the cooling room I asked Joe the obvious question: "If it's so certain that you have a claim for innocence, why haven't the courts, after ten years of considering well-crafted appeals, agreed?" He answered: "It isn't that the courts weren't convinced one way or the other, but that they're bound by the procedural rules they created. It's a court rule that if the defense attorney didn't make proper objections during the trial, then the error cannot be raised on appeal. The second procedural rule states that any new evidence must be raised within twenty-one days of the trial's conclusion, otherwise the review is forever barred. Federal courts must defer to state procedural rules. Because of all this, no court has ever ruled on the merits of my case."

On earlier visits I came to know Giarratano as a serious reader with a strong bent for the literature of nonviolence. I began sending him books by Gandhi, King, Dorothy Day, Dan Berrigan, and others. In one conversation I suggested that if he ever were released from death row, he should become a teacher, perhaps a teacher of nonviolence. Not a bad idea, he said.

A workable idea, it turned out. We strategized. My Center for Teaching Peace would fund a course in the literature of nonviolence, Joe would teach it, and prison officials would sponsor and monitor it. It would not count for parole points. After being transferred from Mecklenburg to a prison in Craigsville, Augusta County, Giarratano approached an assistant warden about making this work. The official, who had been a social worker before taking up corrections, was sympathetic.

The fourteen-week course began in the summer of 1992, with Giarratano as the teacher and *Solutions to Violence* as the main text. Because of his influence among fellow prisoners—having legally fought for them in courts and having triumphed over death row himself—Giarratano was able to recruit the toughest cons to take his course. He wanted to send a message throughout the prison, he told me, that the once-mean guys, the former monsters, are now studying Gandhi, Tolstoy, Thomas Merton, and the others. Nonviolence, he said, is for tough people, the genuinely tough who are brave enough to settle things without using fists or guns.

In January of the following year the first graduation ceremony took place in a large receiving room near the visitors' area. More than one hundred inmates were in the audience. The warden and a half dozen prison officials attended, along with some of the prisoners' family members. I brought a bus load of students from Washington and had sent some money to the warden to pay for food for everyone.

Marie Deans was the commencement speaker. Included in her remarks was this: "The success of the peace-studies program is evaluated by tracking the disciplinary records. Most of the graduates here today have a long history of disciplinary charges for assault or fighting right up to the time they entered the program. Since the program began, not one graduate has been charged." At a graduation ceremony two years later, the warden rose to say exactly the same. He had become the program's strongest backer.

Graduates received peace diplomas. On calling the men to the stage to receive them, I asked each one to say a few words about the course. Few had ever given a speech before. They were ready now. One by one they came forward with the same message: "If I had known about nonviolence when I was a kid, I probably wouldn't be in this place today."

When taking student groups to graduations, the only request I made was that they not ask prisoners what they were in for. Crime was part of their past, not necessarily their present or future. Men who had killed, raped, stolen, and destroyed had a few moments at the ceremonies to be accepted as citizens capable of comebacks, of asking forgiveness and receiving mercy.

After one of the trips, Jennifer Gurney, a senior in my high school class at Bethesda–Chevy Chase High School wrote to the men:

I am grateful to have had the chance to meet all of you. Congratulations on graduating from the course on nonviolence. Before I visited, I was ignorant of the kind of life all of you have to lead, separated from society. I believe that many of us, including myself, take our lives for granted. I also think that the prison system in this country needs drastic reform. Prisons should not be places of violence but of teaching and learning. I hope all of you will continue to study the theories of nonviolence. I know I will.

Ariana Grebe, a classmate, wrote to Giarratano and the men:

Thank you so much for the lovely day. It was the first time I had gone to a prison, and I must admit that I felt

*a little apprehensive. But once I entered the visiting
room and saw everyone mingling I felt more at ease.
I'm so impressed by the commitment you men have
made to find inner peace and deal with your violent
environment. I can't imagine the struggles you must
endure and the opposition you meet. You are deserving
of my admiration and everyone else's. No matter what
you may have done in your past, what you are doing
now is what counts. One of the men who spoke when
he received his certificate struck a chord with me—
about looking within your own heart and how it's the
hardest thing you can do. I agree and I understand. I
recently looked within myself as well.*

At one of the graduations in late 1994 a prisoner—presciently, it turned out—warned that the program's visibility might be its undoing. Governor George Allen had installed a new director of prisons, a minion hellbent on carrying out the state's new policies of longer sentences, infrequent parole, gutting counseling and education programs, and severe punishment in round-the-clock lockdowns. Nationally, this was three-strikes-you're-out time, when such politicians as Senator Phil Gramm called America's prisons "Holiday Inns."

The visibility had indeed increased. NBC Nightly News aired a favorable story. Bob Abernethy did a report from the prison in which he interviewed Giarratano and others in the course. More funds came in, including a three-thousand-dollar grant from the Campaign for Human Development sponsored by the U.S. Catholic Conference.

In the summer of 1995 the peace-studies program was terminated. I was told that officials in the state corrections office in Richmond saw the positive publicity about the program—on NBC News and in newspaper and magazine stories—as negative publicity: what's going on in Virginia? Dirtbag cons sitting around discussing Gandhian theories. Taking classes on peace. What kind of coddling is this?

Giarratano was sent to another prison in the state system. In July authorities returned him to Craigsville. Two months later he was routed from his cell in the predawn hours, shackled and chained, and led to a van that carried him to a local airport, there to board a small plane that would take him to a state prison in Utah.

Transfers like this are routine. One state has a prisoner who is troublesome—he has too much power among inmates, he has access to the media about prison conditions, he is running a cellblock gang—and another state has one too. They swap. Problem solved.

For a while. Once in Utah, Giarratano was able to alert the ACLU in Salt Lake City about abuses to prisoners. He went on a hunger strike. After six months Utah had had enough. Giarratano was dispatched to the Illinois state prison in Joliet. A Virginia official told me he had become "problematic." He declined to offer specifics. I had an idea of the kind of problems Giarratano was creating in the Utah pen. One of its inmates wrote to me:

Dear Colman:

I have been talking with Joe Giarratano since he came here to Utah. One of the main topics has been bettering the situation for teaching prisoners to promote positive growth within themselves. Of course he has told me about the Peace Studies Alternatives to Violence program he had going in Virginia and I am very interested in starting the same program here.

I have written to you with his encouragement to ask for any assistance you might be able to offer me in this endeavor. Like any materials to better prepare myself to bring a comprehensive proposal to the administrators here. There are a few caring individuals I have worked with in the past eleven years of my incarceration here in Utah. And I am quite sure it can all come together.

I have this year to really prepare all this, because I get out of the control unit then and will have direct

*access to all the facilities here. However, I will do all I
can to get the ball rolling from here. The violence level
in this system has been rising fast in the past three to
four years. This is due to the increase of the younger
gang offenders. This has caused an epidemic of racial
separation and tensions. That wasn't really an issue
here in past years. And the system here is responding
by building more and more control units and twisting
the thumbscrews. I personally use my time to work on
self-realization. And as a natural result, the more I
realize self, the more I sympathize with the problems
and hardships of those around me. So I feel a personal
responsibility to do all I can.*

In the summer of 1997 I visited Joe in the Joliet prison, an
aging operation in the center of the small city—named after
Père Joliet, an eighteenth-century Jesuit missionary—an hour
south of Chicago. His spirit was strong. He planned to try to
get a peace-studies course started with the help of a prison
chaplain who was sympathetic to the idea.

Nothing came of it. Giarratano's efforts were seen as agi-
tation. Illinois called Virginia and said to come take him back.

For the past four years Giarratano has been caged in an 8'
x 11' isolation cell in the Red Onion state prison in Pound,
Virginia. Red Onion, in rural southwest Virginia, a seven-hour
drive from Washington, is a supermax facility where inhumane treatment of prisoners is common. *The Washington
Post* reported in April 1999 that "in Red Onion's first nine
months, shots have been fired [at inmates] 63 times." The
paper quoted Ronald Angelone, the state's director of prisons and a champion of supermax pens, on his views about
Red Onion: "It's not a nice place. And I designed it not to be
a nice place."

The prison has no law library, no meaningful job-training
program, and no significant education classes. A directive
states: "Copies or sections of publications, brochures, news-
letters, materials printed off the Internet, or other printed

materials will no longer be allowed or enclosed in incoming correspondence."

For exercise, Giarratano is allowed to move around in a walled concrete area the size of a dog pen. In a letter to me he wrote: "I am strip searched each time I leave the cell for recreation. I am first handcuffed behind the back, legs shackled, placed on a metal dog leash, escorted by two guards—one holding the leash, the other pressing a laser gun to my ribs—and all under the close watch of a guard pointing a shotgun at me from the gun port."

That should be considered soft treatment. In early 2000 Giarratano was confined to his cell twenty-four hours a day, except for three five-minute showers a week. His offense? He retained a mustache, a major violation of the Department of Correction's hair-grooming regulations.

In one of his regular letters—this one on May 7, 2000—Giarratano described his feelings about life at Red Onion:

Generally, I am holding up well under the rigors of supermax segregated confinement, probably better than many. Nevertheless, I know that anyone subjected to this type of ordeal—especially for long durations—does not escape unscathed. I know, in my own experiences here and from past experiences with long-term isolated segregated lockdowns—my years on the row—the tremendous amount of mental concentration it requires just to keep one's head above water. There are times, even now, when I'm not so sure of my own grip on reality. The social isolation, greatly restricted environmental and intellectual stimulation, forced idleness, constant confinement to a small space day after day, being subjected to a constant denial of one's innate humanity and dignity—constantly being treated like an object and not a human being—the total lack of personal privacy, the light bulb on 24 hours a day and living under the constant threat of officially sanctioned violence will, I suppose, take its toll on anyone. More

*and more, I find myself having to turn inward just to
maintain my balance in this madness. Even then, I
must remain on guard against hallucinations, feelings
of suffocation, paranoia, fear, and even rage.*

In the same letter Giarratano included an excerpt from an
1890 Supreme Court decision involving the sensory-depri-
vation isolation of inmates in locked-down cells: "A consid-
erable number of prisoners fell, after even a short time in
confinement, into a semi-fatuous condition, from which it
was next to impossible to arouse them, and others became
violently insane; others still, committed suicide, while those
who stood the ordeal better were not generally reformed, and
in most cases did not recover sufficient mental activity to be
of any subsequent service to the community."

Giarratano has told me that one of the forces that keeps
him from despair, or suicide, is the correspondence he has
with supporters who have not forgotten him. In the spring of
1999 many of them were among the more than two hundred
friends who gathered at a Doubletree hotel dinner in
Charlottesville, Virginia, to honor Giarratano's heroic resistance against the state's courts and the correction department's efforts to crush his spirits.

The dinner was on May 1, the same day that the mayor of
Charlottesville, in a move that no one could recall ever happening anywhere involving a prisoner, declared May 1 Joseph Giarratano Day. The proclamation was meant to pay
homage to a man that many Virginians—on both sides of the
death-penalty issue—believe is innocent. Among those
speaking at the dinner was Judge Robert Merhige, now re-
tired. In a fifteen-minute speech he aligned himself with all
those in the audience who continued to work to win
Giarratano's freedom. Merhige condemned the twenty-one-
day rule.

In late February 2000 the Virginia House of Delegates voted
73-25 on a bill that would end the twenty-one-day rule. The
forty-two Democrats and thirty-two Republicans supporting

the change believed that, finally, Virginia would no longer be the only one of the nation's thirty-eight death-penalty states denying appellate relief for possibly innocent people. Two weeks later the state Senate, lobbied loudly by prosecutors, refused to consider the bill.

Every fall semester at Georgetown Law and my other schools I have my classes read about and discuss the life and thoughts of Joe Giarratano. At Georgetown many students have written their required six-thousand-word papers on his case. Kathleen Phelps began her paper by recalling her initial jolts of fright at the Craigsville prison. Students were passed through security five at a time and led, five by five, into the main reception room filled with prisoners:

> *Suddenly we were the strangers. Several of the men welcomed us warmly. I glanced at my friend Susan and could tell that she had the same thoughts I did: "These are mass murderers. Drug dealers. Rapists. My God, they are so friendly and so unashamed." At this thought, I became ashamed. I was so suspicious, looking into each inmate's face as if I could read there of his crime. As the evening wore on, I got up the courage to talk to several men. I wanted to hear what they had to say. I wondered about living behind walls.*

At one of the graduations Joe Giarratano rose to give a brief welcoming speech. "In spite of our confinement and the violence that surrounds us, we have come to know that we are not helpless. Just as we have contributed to the problem, we just as easily can contribute to the solutions. We all have a role to play in reducing violence."

One of those roles has been taken by Amy Hatfeld. In 1989 she was a senior in my class at Bethesda–Chevy Chase High. Outside of keeping track of her credit cards—she was a champion shopper and wore elegant clothes and jewelry to prove it—and finding a daily parking space at school, she wasn't overburdened with worries, especially not her studies.

So far, she was getting by on her smile. Her life in the bowl of Chevy Chase was full of cherries. In 1989 she came on the field trip to Mecklenburg. While talking to some of the men on death row, she learned that many had no lawyers for the appeals process. The daughter of a lawyer, one who became an administrative law judge in Washington, Amy wondered about the fairness of that. She learned, too, that many of the men were illiterate or semi-illiterate, which was why they held Joe Giarratano in high regard.

In the months following the visit to the prison, Amy had less and less interest in the malls. She began reading the papers for stories about the justice system. In class she moved from the back row to the front. She threw herself into the debates. The next year she was at the University of Michigan, taking classes in government, sociology, and women's studies. She became a campus organizer for a gender-equality program. She graduated summa cum laude. Motivated, she joined Teach for America and served in a middle school in a Hispanic neighborhood in Pasadena, California. She decided to go to law school. I tried persuading her to come to Georgetown. She applied and was easily accepted, as she was at several other high-ranked schools. One of the risks of going to a prestigious law school is ending up at a prestigious law firm. Amy chose the law school at the City University of New York, known for social activism. Few Wall Street or K Street firms set up booths there on Career Day. Amy is now a public-interest lawyer in an impoverished New York City neighborhood. She continues to stay in touch with Joe Giarratano.*

---

* On February 12, 2001, Earl Washington was released from prison. DNA evidence exonerated him. Members of Congress invited him to the Capitol to speak, but Virginia prison officials decreed he could not leave the state. He has six months of parole to serve on an unrelated assault conviction. None of the national news stories about Washington's release from prison mention the life-saving role played by Joe Giarratano. Days before Washington's release, the Virginia legislature moves closer to passing a bill to

The Washington Center

Tom Cruickshank, a senior at Franklin Pierce College in southern New Hampshire, began the semester with a dream internship. Or so he thought. It was the White House. Before his first day Tom's imagination slipped its harness. There he'd be, he pictured, sitting in on policy meetings with the president and the cabinet, taking notes for the position papers he'd be writing for the senior staff, phoning around the country to the offices of governors and mayors to keep the heartland abreast, and writing letters on White House stationery to the folks at home. He'd like to see their faces when the postman brings a letter with "The White House" printed in dark blue on the upper left of the envelope. Just "The White House." No street address. No zip. Total class.

Tom's Mom and Dad in Farmingdale, Long Island, were indeed wildly impressed when the first letter came, bragging to the relatives that—Wow!—their boy had risen to the top. But after a week at the White House, Tom had discovered his true station in life: errand boy, photocopier operator, the one who ordered pizza late into the night, phone message taker for more self-important papercrats and bureaucrats than he could count. Worse, he was not in the White House at all but in a third-floor back room of the Old Executive Office Building. Worse still, he had to listen to his friends who had internships at obscure NGOs gasp when he mentioned the White House and pretend that he had lucked out with the ultimate glamour job.

---

amend the twenty-one-day rule. But it will do nothing to help Giarratano, Dassette, or Payne. *The Washington Post* reported on February 9, 2001: "Only prisoners who have new biological evidence would be eligible to go back to court. New witnesses, fingerprints, ballistic tests and anything unrelated to DNA or blood are excluded from the legislation. . . . A Death Penalty Information Center study shows that DNA tests have freed just 10 of the 93 men released from death row nationwide since 1973. The others relied on other evidence."

I've seen similar deflations before. Tom wanted out. "Stick with it," I said. "You're learning how the gears of government really work, oiled by egos, agendas, power grabs, and occasionally, a decent deed for the public good."

By way of modest rescue, I made arrangements for Tom to spend one day a week at Garrison Elementary. Help some kids with their reading. He caught the White House intern director on a good day and was relieved of his paper-shuffling duties every Thursday. He had no way of knowing, but his service at Garrison would cause a major shift in the direction of his life.

Tom was welcomed at the school by Hassan Abdullah, a second-grade teacher. He is fifty, in his seventh year at Garrison and fifteenth of elementary school teaching. African American, he is a rarity, a minority within a minority. In the faculties of America's 61,165 public elementary schools, only 11 percent are men. Of that, less than 5 percent are blacks. The National Education Association says that "classrooms everywhere are starved for good teachers of color."

Raised in a Baptist family in Washington, Hassan embraced the Muslim faith in 1974 after graduating from the old D.C. Teachers College. "I'm a teacher," he said during a lunch break when I brought students in for a field trip, "because it's God's will. For a long time I tried to avoid going into grade school teaching. I thought that it just wouldn't look right for a man to be in a classroom with little children."

After earning a master's degree in early childhood education and working ten years as a consultant to state and federal school programs, Hassan, obedient to God, was in the classroom. "From what parents have shared with me," he said, "and from my own observations, male teachers—particularly African-American males—are making a dramatic difference in the lives of young developing children. It's because so many come from one-parent homes, and that parent is the mother. A lot of our boys—and girls, too—have not had the nurturing relationship with a male. As a result, my students tend to listen to me. They try to adhere to the classroom rules. There's a difference between boys and girls. If you ask girls to attend to a task, they go right away. With boys, you have to watch them all the way, or they'll deviate. Most of the boys don't seem to respect women, not the way I was raised."

Hassan tells stories about his own male teachers who were positive influences. He knows it is likely he will be remembered that way, too, by many of his Garrison children. He is sad that so few black males are teaching. "If only they knew how valuable they are in an elementary school, they'd be flying here."

Tom Cruickshank, who walked across Europe one summer, isn't black, but he did fly to Garrison every week. And he learned that he is valuable. He turned in a paper that offers further proof that experiential knowledge is what college students both desire and deserve. Parts of it read:

> *When I first stepped into Hassan Abdullah's second-grade classroom, I was greeted with the most polite and well-mannered group of kids I have ever met. Mr. Abdullah was as excited by my being there as the students were. On introducing myself, the children were in awe. I noticed this but I wondered what they were in awe of. Some college boy burnout wearing a sports jacket with a flashy federal pin on the right breast. Sure, they're little kids. Everything intrigues them. But nothing, and I mean nothing, intrigues them as much as Mr. Abdullah. The children love him. He is caring and kind.*
>
> *Our first activity was a group reading session that we do every week. Each student takes turns reading. Some have trouble and some don't, but most of them can read words and make sentences with the exception of one boy. His name is Lawrence. The kids call him Larry. The class became silent when it came his turn to read. The kids began to whisper and shuffle as they realized Larry's reading skills weren't at the level they should be. We skipped him and went on.*

After class, Mr. Abdullah approached me with an embarrassed tone in his voice. He explained how Larry was from an abandoned father. His mother, in her early 20s, worked at a dead end job. She neglected to get up early enough to get Larry to school for the whole month of November. Mr. Abdullah was angry about it. He cursed the boy's mother and shook his head. I realized he cared in his heart about this child. He wants the best for him as if he were his own.

We decided that it was my position to work with Larry as well as the others and make sure they all pass the Stanford 9 reading test. Mr. Abdullah also told me that he appreciates feedback on any learning disabilities any of the students may have: poor eyesight, dyslexia. We've both decided that one girl named Keisha must have her eyes tested. We were pretty pumped up that we could agree on this. Mr. Abdullah just needed a second opinion on her problem.

Since coming to Garrison I have absolutely fallen in love with these kids. I look forward to being with them more than I do the weekends. The one-on-one time I get to spend with these children is so rewarding. For me, volunteer work is always more rewarding than paid work.

When I return to Long Island, I plan on volunteering at Amityville Elementary School. It's a neighborhood as grim as Garrison's. I realize now the importance of good parenting and teaching peace. Although the time I've spent at Garrison is brief, it has truly changed my life.

On returning Tom Cruickshank's paper, I suggest that he tell the folks at home to brag about his being at Garrison Elementary, not the White House.*

---

* On August 22, 2001, Tom Cruickshank phoned to tell me that he has just accepted his first job offer after college as second-grade teacher at a school in Far Rockaway, Queens, New York. He asked for Hassan Abdullah's address, to write him a letter of thanks for giving him refuge.

University of Maryland

Final classes leave me wondering, what have they learned? They've read some, written some. They've shown up, they've paid the university. I gave them full effort, no need for a five-dollar refund.

What they've learned is really knowable only by each student. The course is pass/fail, which is the purest academic joy for me. A relief, as well. No time will be wasted on turning in grades.

Not everyone takes to gradeless learning. A parent phoned a few years ago at the end of the semester. The dialogue went along these lines:

"Professor, how did my daughter do in your course? Her report card just said 'P.'"

"How did your daughter do? I have no idea. You need to ask your daughter."

"But you're her teacher. How did she do?"

"Do you mean what did she learn?"

"No, what was her grade. That's what counts."

"Not in my course. What counts is what a student learns."

"So what did my daughter learn?"

"How would I know? Ask your daughter. She's the only one who knows what she learned."

"But you're the professor."

"Right. And your daughter is your daughter, and your daughter is the student. Ask her what she learned. Have you asked her?"

"No, I don't need to. I look at the report card."

"That just tells you the grade, not what she learned."

"But the 'P' is only a 'P.'"

"Right. She passed."

"That doesn't say how she did."

"I know."

"So how did she do?"

"Ma'am, I'm about to make as solemn a promise to you as I've ever made to any human being. If you ask your daughter what she learned as a student in my class, I promise she will tell you. How do I know? She has a honed talent for honesty—I've seen it in class—and you have great reason to be proud of her."

"Did she make an 'A?' That's what I'd really be proud of."

"No, she made a 'P.'"

"That doesn't tell me anything."

"Your daughter will tell you. Ask her."

The dialogue tapered off, not a syllable too soon for me. It was headed directly into the territory Abbot and Costello covered in their "Who's on First" routine. I wished the mother well and suggested she come audit my course next year if she truly wanted an inkling about what her daughter had learned.

Too slow on the uptake, I should have told her to read Theodore Sizer. While teaching at Brown, where students have the option of a pass/fail grading system, he wrote of "our absolute myopic concern about assessments, grading and evaluation. We have this mania for rating people. It's a plague at the school level. . . . The grade is an end in itself."

I've experimented a few times with tempering this plague. A few years ago at a university, during the first minutes of the first class of the semester, I asked my students, "Is anyone here just to get a grade? If so, announce what grade you want, and you can leave now and never return. I promise at the end of the course I'll turn in the grade you request."

The students were stunned by this unprecedented offer. They cast glances at each other, as if saying, "There's a catch. Be careful." I waited for someone to say, "I'll take an 'A.' Thanks and goodbye."

No one ever left. They all stayed, and I went all out to help them be self-demanding, the effective way to learn. These semesters have been lively semesters, the ones you remember.

The question always in the minds of teachers, as we stand before students prattling on and looking into their faces is, "Are they getting it?" We must know. Yes, of course they're getting it, and I'm here dispensing all this wisdom, like a lord of the heavens sending down water into dry wells. Our professorial hearts go tingle, tingle. Our lives have deep meaning getting deeper.

At American University in the mid-1980s I had a student who came into class late every week. She slipped in quietly, nodded faintly in my direction, and went for the back rows. After five minutes her eyes blanked out. Her face glazed over. She'd put her head back, as if in a trance trying to make contact with outer space beings. Must be a philosophy major, I thought. Then thought number two: she's not within six hemispheres of "getting it."

At semester's end, my back-row dreamer graduated. I had no expectation of ever hearing from her. Five or so years later a letter came. From Morocco. She had joined the Peace Corps. I thought back to her class. She was the last one I would have pegged for the Peace Corps. She was assigned to a small village in the Northern Sahara to teach in a desert elementary school. One day a copy of the *International Paris Herald Tribune* found its way into the teacher's lunch room. The paper was a few weeks old, but the news was still fresh for those who hadn't heard it. She came upon a column of mine. It prompted her to write. She said I probably didn't remember her, she wasn't much of a student, being in her last semester of college, bored numb, and eager to get going. She confessed that she didn't do much reading and connected intellectually with only a few of the theories about nonviolence. But now that she was long gone from the classroom and a teacher herself, many of the ideas from the course were coming back to her. Yes, she said, now that I'm out here involved in a small way in the works of peace and justice, nonviolence does make sense. She was committed to it.

That kind of letter means more than a thousand paychecks ever could. Was she "getting it"? Irrelevant question. It's none of any teacher's business. I tell this story the last class of every semester. Its moral is obvious. Some flowers bloom early and right in front of us. Others bloom late in distant gardens.

I ask all to stay in touch and write from whichever Moroccos they find themselves in.

Oak Hill

Of late, I lack all taste on what columnists, editorial writers, and politicians say about "the black youth problem." The cant is unstomachable, the thinking of its producers unbearable. They might as well try to describe the landscape on the far side of Neptune. What do they know, beyond the repetitious and theoretical, about the lives of prisoners? After three years at Oak Hill—and it is not much, an afternoon a week—I have mood swings between hope and despair. Yes, these kids are reachable. No, come to your senses, they aren't. It's laughable. The political Left says keep trying, these kids can be rehabilitated. Except they have yet to be *habilitated*. The political Right says build more prisons, end parole, and hire more cops for the streets.

The jabber is meaningless to me when I meet with my Oak Hill class. Theories don't matter here. Only comebacks. With six or seven boys gathered round in a circle in the commons room every week, I try only to move them toward thinking about personal responsibility and nudge them beyond the victimization mindset that some of them have. Of course the structures of an economically and racially divided society throw black kids under a bus, leaving them to die or rot. Of course they are victims. Of course they have hard lives. But those aren't ropes that automatically tie their hands and feet into a state of lifelong self-paralysis.

Easy talk for me. What do I say to the run-over kids before me? What credibility do I have, coming from a secure background of unearned benefits and uncounted breaks? The inmates at Oak Hill are as grounded in their identities as I am in mine, with scant overlap. Yet I have never had even a hint of hostility thrown at me by the kids here. When coming in each week, I make it a point to shake hands with each one of them, and shake hands again on leaving. I have learned names. A few of them begin to call me Peace Man.

I've been thinking that perhaps I make too much of our differences. If it doesn't come up in our classes—and it rarely has—I should let it pass. Mutual acceptance has evolved. Showing up week after week is a positive message the Oak Hill kids pick up instinctively. That, and coming in with relevant literature.

Today I come with an essay by Carl Upchurch, an excerpt from his book *Convicted in the Womb: One Man's Journey from Prisoner to Peacemaker*. I've met Carl a few times, most recently in Denver where we were both speaking at a conference for elementary and high school teachers. In his mid-fifties, he has a bulky frame, a sonorous voice, and a relaxed mien. He is physically powerful yet personally meek—not an everyday combination. Raised in an impoverished South Philadelphia neighborhood, he was one more street thug handy with guns and knives, with a body gashed with scars he carried like battle ribbons.

It was during a stretch at Western State Penitentiary in Pennsylvania that his recovery began. He took classes, an opportunity

> to go to school that came along just when I was ready to understand that education is a gift. . . . I began to see the world in a new way. In the context of the stories, biographies, autobiographies, poetry, and history that I read, I began to evaluate my own life and my many shortcomings. I was challenged by a wide range of authors to examine the behaviors that had brought me to this place of despair. And eventually I glimpsed my humanity, small fragments of my connectedness to a wider universe of common decency. This connectedness served as a powerful reminder of the potential salvageability of self. It was in me at birth but was buried by poverty, racism, social inequities, anger and hopelessness.

The boy I ask to read this passage moves haltingly from one word to another. He stumbles over words like "eventually" and "humanity" and stops dead at "connectedness" and "salvageability." I wonder if this writing is so far above the class that it serves only to discourage them. Or will it challenge some of them to dig in? I can't really know. It's up to each of the boys to choose.

Four paragraphs later the language is clearer.

Change comes from within, and before we can change the world around us, we must change ourselves one by one. We must look in the mirror and acknowledge our responsibility for our lives. "I'm the one carrying a gun." "I'm the one shooting dope into my arm." "I'm the one getting drunk everyday." "I'm the one who dropped out of school." "I'm the one who would rather steal than work." "I'm the one who uses violence, or threats of violence, to make my way through the world." "I'm the one setting an example for the children around me." "I'm the one killing my brother." "My behavior contributes to my niggerization."

The last word, I explain, means negative, self-destructive behavior—ducking personal responsibility and blaming everyone else for the messes our lives have become.

Is Upchurch getting through? I wonder. This isn't a Billy Graham revival hour, where the sinners come forward to repent and be saved. For some of the boys the essay we are reading is probably little more than another exercise in boredom—words on a page, pages from a book, a book written by a stranger whose life is elsewhere, like all the other lives outside the prison fences. But for others in the class I think some sinking-in could be happening; they're the "one" Upchurch talks about.

On leaving, one of the boys, who sees that I have Carl's book with me, asks if he can borrow it. I'm surprised. This boy is the one with the most seethe in him, who never shakes hands with me, who often declines to read aloud, who mocks others in the class when they speak honestly, who sometimes walks out of class. I give him the book. I show him the title page, which has an inscription from Carl to me. "You know this man?" the boy asks. "Yes," I answer. "We're friends."

For the first time he offers his hand to me, gripping mine with a firm shake.

Semester's End

A Few of the Many Who "Got It"

At semester's end, before wishing my students well—"Don't go out and change the world, keep the world from changing you"—I take some moments for a reading from Albert Schweitzer's "Reverence for Life." It has nourished me often, an essay on idealism and the drive to keep it alive no matter the battering the world will soon enough deliver.

The core lines of the essay:

No one has the right to take for granted his own advantages over others in health, in talents, in ability, in success, in a happy childhood or congenial home conditions. One must pay a price for all these boons. What one owes in return is a special responsibility for other lives.

As the "booned" students leave, I look at them and wonder which ones I will remember, which ones I will hear from as the years pass, which ones will never waver from believing that the good life is incompatible with the violent life, which ones will remember me as a teacher who wanted only to rouse their passions for justice and rally their gifts for peacemaking, which ones will I keep track of and think to myself—they understood what the course was about, they "got it."

My memory brims with stories of former students.

Tara Lee

After I wrote a column on the immorality of the U.S. invasion of Panama in 1989, and some efforts by women officers to get more combat time, a reader wrote scathingly to say that my views on things military were imbecilic. That bordered on flattery compared with the usual tone of letters from military supporters. The letter was well-crafted, displaying an ease with language and fair-minded argument. It was from Tara Lee, a midshipman in her third year at the U.S. Naval Academy in Annapolis. I arranged to have the letter printed in the Style section of *The Washington Post*, next to my reply. Wanting a photograph to go with the exchange, a *Post* editor asked me to go to the Naval Academy to pose with Tara. I did, with the photographer placing us next to a two-ton gunboat cannon. "Stay calm," Tara joked. "It's not loaded." I liked her cheeriness.

After the exchange of letters ran in the *Post*, Tara phoned to thank me for getting her into print. She was an English major at the Academy. Her professors were impressed, and a few of them envious that she was now a published writer. In passing, I suggested that if she wanted to push herself to learn more about nonviolence—her *Post* letter argued that it was a noble theory but that national defense needed more than noble theories—she should come over to Georgetown Law as my guest and take my course. I offered the invitation with no thought it would be accepted.

Opening day next semester, Tara Lee was there. She had become my most unlikely student. Short of psychiatric evaluations and an emergency meeting of the Joint Chiefs, she had to go through a half-dozen channels to win permission to make the weekly trip. She became a popular member of the class and could be endearingly ironic about her weekly adventure. At the Academy, she said, fellow midshipmen saw her as consorting with the enemy—the subversive, long-haired Left at Georgetown Law—while at the law school, where she would show up in her whites, some of her classmates viewed her as sunk in military conservatism.

As always, the labels were hollow. Tara Lee, a Tampa native, had a refreshingly open mind. I wondered more than once during the semester where the course would take her.

Five years after leaving the Academy—she had invited me to the graduation to meet her parents—Tara called. Stationed at a Southern California naval base, she had been going to law school at night and had earned her juris doctor degree from the University of San Diego Law School. She specialized in public-interest law and worked at a children's advocacy institute. While volunteering at a women's homeless shelter in the law school's clinic, she represented abused children. "You can leverage change with a law degree," she said. "Kids are the most undefended people in America."

Jim McGovern

In 1984 at American University, Jim McGovern was a reflective and politically alert student working on a master's degree. In my class he picked up nuances in the readings that others missed by miles. He saw connections between the moral reasonings of Gandhi, Tolstoy, and the others and the political issues of the day. After two or three weeks I discovered why. He was an administrative assistant to a congressman, Rep. Joseph Moakley, a Boston Democrat and housemate on Capitol Hill of Tip O'Neill. U.S. military aid to the government of El Salvador came up in class once. The assassination of Archbishop Oscar Romero had occurred four years earlier, on March 24, 1980. El Salvador is right here in Washington, someone in the class said.

Refugees have made the Adams Morgan section of the city a haven for families fleeing the war. "Some of them," I said, "are being sheltered by Carmelite Sisters in a convent near the U.S. Capitol. Volunteers are welcomed there."

One of those who went was Jim McGovern. He listened to the women's stories on the brutality and misery they endured in El Salvador and their fears of never returning home. He passed along the horrors to Joe Moakley and others in

Congress. Funding the war was no longer another foreign-policy abstraction. War victims were living a mile from congressional offices.

After earning his graduate degree from American, Jim became one of the most knowledgeable staff people in Congress on El Salvador. He organized congressional trips, many of them high-risk ventures because he would go to San Salvador a week ahead to do the advance work. American nuns, journalists, and labor organizers had been slain. In time Joe Moakley, counseled by Jim McGovern, became both the voice of the poor in El Salvador and the sternest critic of U.S. military aid. Not long before his death in 1980, Archbishop Romero pleaded with President Jimmy Carter—"Christian to Christian"—not to send military aid to El Salvador. Send food, clothing, and medicine, if you want to help, but, please, no weapons. Romero was ignored. At the time of his assassination, he was the eleventh Catholic priest killed in three years. Members of the Salvadoran death squads, many of them trained at the School of the Americas, Ft. Benning, Georgia, had a favorite slogan: "Be patriotic, kill a priest." Beginning with Carter, billions of dollars in weapons—$6 billion is the most cited amount—was to flow to the Salvadoran government, a major violator of human rights, over the next ten years. Two years later, in 1982, Carter, suddenly a world citizen, saw things differently: "I think the government of El Salvador is one of the bloodthirstiest in the hemisphere."

That was the same assessment Jim McGovern made in the 1980s, and one that his boss, Joe Moakley, would also arrive at on his trips to the embattled country subsumed by U.S. weapons. He is credited with persuading Congress to cut off funding in the early 1990s.

After a decade of laboring for Moakley, Jim decided it was his turn. He resigned and returned to Worcester, Massachusetts, his hometown. In early 1994 he announced his candidacy for the open seat in Congress vacated by Rep. Joseph Early. Of the three Democrats in the primary, Jim finished last, winning less than 10 percent of the vote. A Republican,

Peter Blute, was elected. Jim returned to Washington and his job with Moakley. A year later he went home to Worcester for another try. Even the friendliest of handicappers told him he was at best a long shot sure to get longer. Eleven months before the election, scheduled for November 1996, Jim started showing up at every shopping center, every town meeting, every civic luncheon, every newsroom, every neighborhood, and every site where voters gathered. The Democratic Party pros decreed he had no chance and gave him little money to campaign. Beating the incumbent was seen as so unlikely that no Democrat ran in the primary. Each of the seven largest newspapers in the district endorsed Blute, some glowingly. The *Boston Globe* supported him.

Confident of victory, Blute and his handlers wanted to have a bit of sport with Jim McGovern, convinced that they were about to trounce him. They wanted to remind voters just how dangerously to the left he had been. Jim's major offense was taking a delegation from Congress to Cuba to dialogue with Fidel the Infidel, the despot himself. On Halloween a week before election day, Blute hired a local actor to dress up like Castro—army fatigues, black beard, cigar, boots—and stand at the main intersection in downtown Worcester during rush hours holding a large sign saying in block letters: VOTE FOR JIM McGOVERN.

The stunt was seen as so foul that voters retaliated against Blute and voted for Jim 53%-47%. He has been in Congress ever since, so cherished by the citizens that in the 2000 election he ran unopposed. About his opponent's Castro caper, Jim had the last laugh. "It helped get out my Catholic vote," he told me. "I said to the voters that if the pope can go to Cuba and talk to Fidel, so can I."

As a college student Jim McGovern had the markings of a man afire with justice. When others would head to Cancun or Lauderdale for spring break, he would spend more time at the women's homeless shelter or working the congressional offices to spread information about Latin America. He is much the same now, except his concern is about the escalating

U.S. involvement in Colombia. When current students ask me who I admire in Congress, I tell them stories about Jim McGovern. When they ask me who there knows the most solutions to the violence in Latin America, again I tell them, "Go talk to Jim McGovern."

Chappell Marmon

In thirteen years of teaching 7:30 A.M. classes at Bethesda–Chevy Chase High School, I received no paycheck. But I was lavishly compensated by letters from students years later. One, written on April 23, 1999, two days after the shootings at Columbine, was from Chappell Marmon, who studied at Brown after B–CC. She wrote:

Dear Colman,

Over the past few days since the shooting in Colorado, I have been trying to make sense of a lot of things. I have been contemplating the violence of our society, and trying to think about what I can do to change it. One thing I keep coming back to is the need to teach about peace and conflict resolution in the schools. In the last couple of days, I have been recalling our class at B–CC. I am realizing what an impact it had on me. It is not that the idea changed me radically all at once, but that the ideas I was exposed to in class gave me options I hadn't had before. Suddenly the options of opposing the death penalty, of being a vegetarian, of resisting complacency, and of finding alternatives to violence were mine. They are still mine and it has taken me years to take a real position on them. I wonder whether the students in Colorado would have done what they did if they had known about, and felt entitled to, such options.

Another thing I remember about the class was that we always had the chance to really have it out with others whom we disagreed with on the issues. I remember practically screaming across the room at Tom Duffy, and him screaming back at me. We became friends. We certainly couldn't hate each other after having such intense exchanges. I had looked him in the eye and felt him as a person, and he had done the same with me. We could never have killed one another.

I think that had the Columbine students had the chance to get to know each other, to argue with each other about issues that touched all their lives, they wouldn't have had to depend on labels and group designations like "athlete" or "Goth" or "preppy" to decide whether or not they had respect for the life of a fellow student.

I think you're right when you argue that we should start teaching kindergartners about the philosophies of Gandhi and Martin Luther King, Jr. We should be taking eighth graders into prisons and soup kitchens, and we should be teaching high schoolers mediation and conflict resolution.

I hope that I can work toward making peace studies classes like yours a part of every child's learning experience.

I just wanted to take the time to let you know that amid all the feelings of helplessness and sadness I feel after Tuesday's events your class has stood out as a beacon of hope.

And as a guiding star. Thank you so much for expanding my mind and helping me form a vision of where we need to go and what I need to do to help us get there. I hope you never stop doing what you are doing.

Love,
Chappell

For the past two years Chappell Marmon has been teaching English and social studies at a high school—in Colorado.

Lexie Tillotson

During my first year at School Without Walls in 1982, my most independent-minded student was a sixteen-year-old girl with flowing golden hair, wanderlust in her eyes, and impatience in her heart. Some days she wore no shoes. She liked back-row seats; there she hunkered down and read paperbacks when the class discussion bored her. Often she would leave the class halfway through, loping out the door with a breezy "goin' to see my shrink."

This was Lexie Tillotson, daughter of a Harvard father and Vassar mother. She had been booted out of a private girl's school for swigging booze in the bathroom between classes. Now she was at Walls, not yet in full rebellion but merrily on the way to it. I never knew whether she chose to be in my class or was dumped into it by a guidance counselor who thought some peace talk would straighten out Lexie, or at least get her to clip her hair and wear shoes.

In class one afternoon, a line from Gandhi came up: "Poverty is the worst form of violence." Lexie dropped her paperback and stared at the essay on Gandhi that carried those words. Later in the class I reminded the students of Simone Weil's thought: "The love of our neighbor means in all its fullness simply being able to say to him, 'what are you going through?' and then acting on the answer." Love is a command to action, not a mere emotion.

Lexie took the words of Gandhi and Weil to heart. On the paved playground behind the school was a small, clapboard, one-story, single-room building. With wooden planks supporting the roof over a porch, it resembled a sharecropper's home in the rural South. It was a toolshed for the school's maintenance man. Students dubbed the building Smoke House. It had become the hangout for a few of the kids who needed a drag between classes. Lexie often spoke in class about the homeless people she saw on the sidewalks as she walked to school. She began speaking to them as well as listening. She was finding out what they were going through.

In time she came to know the street people living on the sidewalks and heat grates near Walls as human beings. Society's untouchables, supposedly off limits to schoolgirls, had become people with stories.

Lexie's observations prompted me to ask the students to write a reflection paper on what might happen in their household if, after school one day, they came in the front door with a homeless person and suggested to the family that he or she be welcomed as a guest for the next few weeks. The papers came back, ranging from both parents having heart attacks to parents writing a check for the homeless person and taking him or her to the nearest shelter.

Lexie had her own plan. It was Smoke House. With a friend, she came one night to jimmy open a steel-screen window on the front of the building. Next day she passed word to the street people that squatter's rights were theirs if they wanted them. They did. From mid-September to early December the heatless Smoke House served as a shelter for five men and one woman.

Lexie served as the unofficial host.

Her hospitality lasted only those three months. Complaints from neighbors whose condos lined the side of the Walls playground brought the police in one night to roust the six homeless people.

Lexie phoned me, weeping uncontrollably over what the cops had done. I came to Smoke House the next morning. Lexie was waiting. Padlocks sealed the door, and the windows were nailed shut. It was too late to protect Smoke House. By now school officials were siding with the police and the neighbors. Homeless people must not be allowed around schoolchildren.

Lexie Tillotson caught all the angles. It was another bum's rush, except this time she was seeing one up close. I wondered if it would make her cynical. Or if she felt helpless. Or had she learn experientially what she never could have learned theoretically, that she had the power within herself to be a loving person who acted on the answers?

I had no way of knowing right then. Lexie went off to college in California, with her hair unclipped and not bringing extra shoes. She went to law school, earned a degree, and now thirty-five, is as committed as ever to the philosophy of service she practiced so well and so defiantly as a schoolgirl.

Fred Werner

Fred Werner was a student at Bethesda–Chevy Chase High in 1990. In class he was the kind of boy some teachers would find abrasive but that I relish: ever ready to disagree, to rethink a belief or two, and to savor open-minded debate, the hotter the better. If anyone—even the whole class—became rankled that was fine, too. I can't help but have kindly feelings about students like this. It doesn't overly matter what conclusions are reached at their age, only that the reaching be full-hearted and continue on.

Fred went on to the University of Michigan and then, to the surprise of many, joined the Peace Corps. I couldn't have been happier. Every semester of every class for twenty years I have touted the Peace Corps and have had students read the essay on idealism in our text by Sargent Shriver.

Fred was dispatched to Bolivia. In his letters to me he described Miska Mayu, a village in the Andes that had no electricity, phones, or running water except for a few communal spigots. "My work here," he wrote, "consists of teaching environmental education to first and fifth graders and working with farmers to introduce soil-conservation techniques. Of the latter, most of them are low-tech solutions, like terracing, that their ancestors were using thousands of years ago before the Spaniards arrived."

He didn't know it, but Fred was also teaching some North American high school and college students: the ones to whom I read his letters. His words stir thoughts—about service, immersion in another culture, seeing connections between Schweitzer's words and the actions of a Fred Werner, someone like them in most ways. When he returned home to

Bethesda—while he was away I had his younger brother and sister in my classes—I had Fred come in and talk with the students about his service in Bolivia. He did more than talk. He dressed in the garb of the Miska Mayu villager, including a conical hat that Harpo Marx might have worn.

Fred Werner is now at Cornell, in the last stages of earning a doctorate in tropical conservation.

Epilogue

The art of teaching is the art of assisting discovery.
—PABLO CASALS

I've loved being a teacher. It may have happened a few times, but I can't recall ever leaving a class, whether a weekly three-hour seminar or a daily gathering for fifty minutes, without feeling an intense exhilaration. Connections, often undefinable, were made. Possibilities, some dim and some obvious, were visible. Coming to the craft in my mid-forties and not being contractually tied to one school have been blessings. I had a professional life elsewhere, a commitment to newspapering that gave me an income, which meant that teaching could be financially pressureless. Money wasn't involved. If I failed, so what. I could walk away. If it came naturally, I could push on.

When having an occasional doubt that my pushing was the best, I thought back to my boyhood and two teachers I've carried in my heart in special ways as models.

Bernie Shulman

"If only one-twentieth of what's been said here tonight is true," mused the amusing Bernie Shulman before a dinner audience of one hundred on hand for his retirement party, "then maybe I shouldn't be retiring after all."

The crack drew a laugh, one of many that February evening in 1988 at a restaurant in Glen Head, New York. An English

133

teacher and guidance counselor for thirty-eight years at North Shore High School in a Long Island village between Sea Cliff and Glen Head, Bernie Shulman was lavished with perhaps as many laudatory adjectives as ever were uttered on one occasion by local orators.

I was a lavisher from afar, returning in sonship to my hometown both as a native and a prodigal—to repay debts to Bernie as an educator and restate feelings for him as a beloved friend.

He was my senior-year English teacher in 1956. Physically, he had the lank of a 6'4" frame, moving it around the classroom as though he were a road show. Intellectually, his mind had a rare lightsomeness that transformed the most ponderous texts into understandable prose. The message of his infectious love of literature couldn't be missed: if an ordinary Joe like me can work up a bead or two of sweat for Shakespeare or Milton, then the masters can change your minds, too. Give them a chance.

Most of us did. By 1956, Bernie, with a master's degree from New York University, had been teaching for a few years. He knew when to be flexible, when to come on hard. Whatever he meant to others he has touched in nearly four decades of teaching, he was for me at seventeen a kind-hearted thrower of ropes. I was sinking academically, pulled down by the cement of too many report card F's, D's, and Incompletes in algebra, geometry, biology, physics, and other required tortures.

"Kid, you have a problem," Bernie told me. "You may not get out of this place. Let's figure something out."

We did. Noticing that I had been turning in long papers—far longer than anyone else—and had been devouring all he had to offer in his English class, Bernie arranged that I do extra writing for him. He'd supply the extra credits and maybe at the end of the year they would add up. With a diploma I could slip out, praying ardently that no one would ever discover that I didn't know about geometric bonkazoids and hypotanoids or how many muscles are on the hind legs of formaldehyded frogs.

For the rest of that year I wrote about one thousand words a night: essays, short stories, poems, and prose excesses that can now be called, with minor pain, adolescent disgorgings of words. Bernie would take anything. The papers would come back a day or two later, sometimes with surgical editing, other times with such tersenesses as "Come off it," "You don't really believe this, do you?" and an occasional "Not bad."

Bernie's philosophy of education, at least as I benefited from it, is one that the academic mahatmas would dismiss as permissive. I should have been made to suffer through math and science courses. Bernie would say "bullbleep"; if a kid is fired up about writing, or about any subject, including math or science, then the school's highest function is to fan the flames, not smother them under the blanket of requirements.

For a year Bernie fanned. The copy I gave him became flammables that still burn. In the past thirty-five years of newspaper and magazine writing, I've averaged two thousand words a week, in the range of 100,000 words a year and one million a decade. One of these years I may get a job, at least if Mark Twain, one of Bernie's favorites, had it right: "Work is what you do when you'd rather be doing something else." Which means I've never worked. It was play that memorable senior year with Bernie, and it's play today.

On my most recent visit to Long Island—two days exchanging views on peace education with students and teachers at Friends Academy in Locust Valley—I stayed with Bernie and his wife, Elsie, a piano teacher, in Old Brookville. Still wary of guff, he let me have it with the same "come off its" he zinged me with nearly a half century before.

I kept notes from Bernie's talk at his retirement dinner. Whether seen as his parting shots or as shots in the arm, these were among them:

+ "The choice of courses for high school students should not be state-mandated. The New York State Regents Action Plan is an example of Mandate Madness."

- "Kids who don't want to go to school, or who disrupt, should be given a variety of alternatives—from CCC-type activities, vocational schools, internships with business and industry, halfway houses or drug rehab centers, state and federally supported."
- "Lawyers should not be allowed into the schoolhouse. Disagreements on salaries, promotions, discipline, and curriculum would have to be settled within the school community."
- "All curricula should include volunteer service in a hospital, senior citizens' home, or hospice," backed up by "field trips to jails, cancer wards, slum areas, and schools for the mentally retarded."

On the journey back to Washington from Glen Head I had time to realize—it took more than three decades to sink in—that this learned, sociable, and fully lovable man was trying to teach me, and all the others who passed through his classes, not only an appreciation of literature but also math. Add peace where there's none, subtract violence when you see it, multiply love when you can, and divide hate when you must. No other math matters.

Marye Eroh

For her first year of teaching after earning a degree in education from New Paltz (New York) State University and then a master's from NYU, Marye Eroh came to Glen Head Elementary School. At twenty-five she was as slender as a model, with a smile that exuded all the charm and cheer my fourth-grade class could want. We boys took turns falling in love with her, ever on sentry duty to pick up signals who she favored most of all. For a time, I knew—absolutely knew with no doubts—she favored *me*.

Early in the fall she pulled me aside and asked if I could do some favors for her. Like wash her car on weekends, I thought. Sure, definitely. I'd be up to something macrocosmic like that, not a low-level chore like banging the erasers clean after school.

Or maybe it was a high-level responsibility—being a walker for her dog, coming over on weekends to her house.

No, the favor was grander than those. She wanted me to go up the hill during recess to the post office to get her mail. She had a boyfriend, Al, who went to Georgia Tech and was always writing letters.

Marye Eroh was in love with someone else? That thought was crushing enough, but worse, now I was to be the errand boy to pick up my rival's letters?

Nothing to do but go get the mail every day and prove I was more worthy of my teacher's love than Al from Georgia Tech, whoever he might be. Soon enough, though, fall sports kicked in, and wondering where Marye Eroh's affections were directed seemed less and less an urgency than my learning how to shoot lay-ups with either hand.

It was in class one day that this young teacher singled me out to do another favor. It came during composition class, a fleeting moment that let me know that my teacher truly did love me.

"Take out a blank piece of paper," she instructed. We were to write a descriptive paragraph on either a person we'd met recently or something that had happened in our neighborhood in the last month.

In less than five minutes I'd put down a dozen sentences and was on the way to setting the fourth-grade record for the longest paragraph ever. Across the room one of my pals sat tapping his pencil and rubbing his rapidly sweating forehead. His paper was blank. Not a word had come. It was an obvious case of early writer's block. After more pencil tapping he went up to Miss Eroh's desk and explained his troubles. Only a few seats away, I overheard her reply: "Here's what you can do. Go over next to Colman. He'll show you how to get started. He's very good with words and sentences."

That last line overwhelmed me. Marye Eroh, idol of all fourth graders, thinks I'm good at writing. Wow. I've been on a high ever since.

Thank you, Bernie. Thank you, Marye. What I owe you, I've been paying to my students.

Select Bibliography on Peace

The literature of peace is vast. Every home should have a peace library. Every person should be reading a peace book. The following is a sampling of the literature. The list is well short of comprehensive and represents only a small percentage of what has been written.

Ackerman, Peter, and Jack Duvall. *A Force More Powerful: A Century of Nonviolent Conflict.* New York: St. Martin's Press, 2000.

Adams, Judith Porter. *Peacework: Oral Histories of Women Peace Activists.* Boston: Twayne Publishers, A Division of G. K. Hall & Co., 1990.

Alonso, Harriet Hyman, Charles Chatfield, and Louis Kriesberg, eds. *Peace as a Women's Issue: A History of the U.S. Movement for World Peace and Women's Rights.* Syracuse, N.Y.: Syracuse University Press, 1993.

Altman, Nathaniel. *The Nonviolent Revolution: A Comprehensive Guide to Ahimsa—the Philosophy of Dynamic Harmlessness.* Dorset, Great Britain: Element Books Limited, 1998.

Berrigan, Daniel. *To Dwell in Peace: An Autobiography.* San Francisco: Harper & Row Publishers, 1987.

Chatfield, Charles, ed. *Peace Movements in America.* New York: Schocken Books, 1973.

Coles, Robert. *The Moral Intelligence of Children.* New York: Penguin Putnam, 1998.

Cornell, Thomas C., Robert Ellsberg, and Jim Forest, eds. *A Penny a Copy: Readings from* The Catholic Worker. Maryknoll, N.Y.: Orbis Books, 1995.

Dear, John, S.J. *The Sacrament of Civil Disobedience.* Baltimore, Md.: Fortkamp Publishing Co., 1994.

Dellinger, David. *Revolutionary Nonviolence: Essays.* Garden City, N.Y.: Anchor Books, Doubleday & Company, 1971.

Diamond, Louise. *The Peace Book: 108 Simple Ways to Create a More Peaceful World.* Berkeley, Calif.: Conari Press, 2001.

Douglass, James W. *The Non-Violent Cross: The Theology of Revolution and Peace.* New York: The Macmillan Company, 1969.

Drew, Naomi. *Peaceful Parents, Peaceful Kids: Practical Ways to Create a Calm and Happy Home.* New York: Kensington Books, 2000.

Gara, Larry, and Lenna Mae Gara. *A Few Small Candles: War Resisters of World War II Tell Their Stories.* Kent, Ohio: The Kent State University Press, 1999.

Hallock, Daniel. *Hell, Healing and Resistance: Veterans Speak.* Farmington, Pa.: The Plough Publishing House of the Bruderhof Foundation, 1998.

Harris, Ian M. *Peace Education.* Jefferson, N.C.: McFarland and Co., 1998.

Hentoff, Nat. *Peace Agitator: The Story of A. J. Muste.* New York: The Macmillan Company, 1963.

Holmes, Robert L. *Nonviolence in Theory and Practice.* Belmont, Calif.: Wadsworth Publishing Co., 1990.

Krieger, David, and Frank Kelly. *Waging Peace II: Vision and Hope for the Twenty-first Century, An Anthology of Essays.* Chicago, Ill.: The Noble Press, 1992.

Laffin, Arthur J., and Anne Montgomery, eds. *Swords into Plowshares: Nonviolent Direct Action for Disarmament, Peace, Social Justice.* Marion, S.D.: Fortkamp Publishing, 1996.

Lantieri, Linda, and Janet Patti. *Waging Peace in Our Schools.* Boston: Beacon Press, 1996.

Lynd, Staughton, and Alice Lynd. *Nonviolence in America: A Documentary History.* Maryknoll, N.Y.: Orbis Books, 1995.

Mananzan, Mary John, Mercy Amba Oduyoye, Elsa Tamez, J. Shannon Clarkson, Mary C. Grey, and Letty M. Russell, eds. *Women Resisting Violence: Spirituality for Life.* Maryknoll, N.Y.: Orbis Books, 1996.

McSorley, Richard T., S.J. *My Path to Peace and Justice: An Autobiography.* Marion, S.D.: Fortcamp Publishing, 1996.

Merton, Thomas. *The Nonviolent Alternative.* New York: Farrar, Straus & Giroux, 1980.

Merton, Thomas, ed. *Gandhi on Nonviolence: A Selection from the Writings of Mahatma Gandhi.* New York: New Directions Publishing, 1964.

Moorehead, Caroline. *Troublesome People: The Warriors of Pacifism.* Bethesda, Md.: Adler & Adler Publishers, 1987.

Nagler, Michael N. *The Search for a Nonviolent Future.* Berkeley, Calif.: Berkeley Hills Books, 2001.

Nolt, John. *Down to Earth: Toward a Philosophy of Nonviolent Living.* Washburn Tenn.: Earth Knows Publications, 1995.

O'Gorman, Angie. *The Universe Bends toward Justice: A Reader on Christian Nonviolence in the U.S.* Philadelphia, Pa.: New Society Publishers, 1990.

Seeley, Robert. *The Handbook of Nonviolence: An Encyclopedia of Pacifism.* Westport, Conn.: Lawrence Hill & Co., 1986.

Shannon, William H. *Seeds of Peace: Contemplation and Non-Violence.* New York: The Crossroad Publishing Co., 1996.

Sharp, Gene. *The Dynamics of Nonviolent Action: Part Three.* Boston, Mass.: Porter Sargent Publishers, 1973.

True, Michael. *An Energy Field More Intense Than War: The Nonviolent Tradition and American Literature.* Syracuse, N.Y.: Syracuse University Press, 1995.

Vanderhaar, Gerald A. *Active Non-Violence: A Way of Personal Peace.* Mystic, Conn.: Twenty-Third Publications, 1990.

Zinn, Howard. *Declarations of Independence: Cross-examining American Ideology.* New York: HarperCollins Publishers, 1990.